"Every parent wants to disciple his or her kids well. Most of us think we have more time, but what if we don't? What if today is what matters and tomorrow isn't promised? Reading Chris Swain's words on discipling our kids in the faith felt like a commentary on a life well-lived. It would be easy to romanticize his final words on discipleship and see them as unattainable, but Swain didn't write that way. He wrote as a parent in the trenches, providing accessible and encouraging tools for parents to use with their kids. I only wish we had more from him. His final work is a gift to parents, like me, who desperately want their kids to know that they love them and God loves them."

COURTNEY REISSIG, Author, *Teach Me to Feel: Worshiping Through the Psalms in Every Season of Life*

"Christian parenting is discipleship. There is nothing more precious than discipling our children—and Chris helps and equips us to do that carefully and intentionally."

ED DREW, Founder, Faith in Kids; Author, *Meals with Jesus*

"A master class in helping us lead our families well. With each word you read, you hear his voice. We must get it right at home; read and obey."

JOHNNY M. HUNT, Senior Vice President, North American Mission Board, SBC

"Much ink has been spilled on parenting and how to raise children. That's not this book. Chris doesn't provide formulas for obedience or discipline. What he provides is a book about intentionally investing in your child through things like love, connection, and prayer—all things that can easily get lost when you just want your child to stop throwing a temper tantrum or leaving their socks all over the house. It's a book about helping both children and parents grow to be more like Jesus—which at the end of the day is what discipleship is all about."

CHRYSTIE COLE, Author, *A Woman's Words; Redeeming Sexuality;* and *Body Matters*

"An inheritance is what you leave for the next generation. A legacy is what you leave in the next generation. As Chris poured out his heart in this book, he truly left a legacy. As you read this book, you will be inspired and equipped to reach and disciple the next generation."

DALE HUDS'

"Get ready for a double dose of the profound and the practical. Let Chris point the way to becoming the spiritual guide you were born to be!"

WILL MANCINI, Founder, Future Church Company; Author, *Future Church*

"*Write It on Their Hearts* is the practical resource that so many parents are looking for. I was always blown away by how intentional, yet simple, Chris's discipleship lifestyle was with his kids. This book captures both the deep insights and the practical applications that he lived out so well. This book is simple, yet powerful. Putting these principles into practice is simple enough to do this week, but powerful enough to change the trajectory of your family."

VICK GREEN, Executive Director, Replicate Ministries

"Parents need easy wins in this post-Christian culture. Chris offers a practical playbook to help parents disciple their kids through easy-to-achieve daily routines. With each new page, parents will feel more confident to step into their God-ordained role of being a "Deuteronomy 6" mom or dad."

RON HUNTER JR., PHD, D6 Conference Director; Author, *The DNA of D6: Building Blocks of Generational Discipleship*

"Parents, this is a must-read! What a tremendous resource to foster the spiritual roots of our children. No simple short cuts but a doable, intentional process that can open a child's heart to the Father."

KATHY FERGUSON LITTON, Director, Planter Spouse Development, North American Mission Board

"As parents, God doesn't call us to be perfect, but he does want us to be good stewards of what he has entrusted to us. Embrace the principles and advice Chris shares here and you will know you are stewarding your role as parent well."

KEVIN EZELL, President, North American Mission Board, SBC

"*Write It on Their Hearts* is an outstanding book on equipping parents to teach their children to walk with God and live out their faith in the world today. Every church across this nation needs to teach this book to their families, and then get it into the hands of every parent in their church."

DR. RONNIE W. FLOYD, Author; Pastor Emeritus, Cross Church, Arkansas

"Most Christian parents know it's their responsibility to disciple their own children. However, very few actually know how to do it. Thankfully, Chris Swain provided this extremely relevant and practical book for all of us. It's a must-have for every parent, grandparent, and guardian. I'll personally be using this book and gifting it to others.

SHANE PRUITT, National Next Gen Director, North American Mission Board; Author, 9 *Common Lies Christians Believe*

"*Write It on Their Hearts* is a clear example of Chris's dedication and commitment to helping families raise their children to love and follow Christ. This book will serve as a great resource in parenting. Chris gives practical insights that are easy to follow while pointing parents to the Father's love."

ERIC GEIGER, Senior Pastor, Mariners Church, Irvine, California

"You will want to read *Write It on Their Hearts* and put what you learn into practice. In doing so, you are making an eternal impact and leaving a legacy with the children the Lord has entrusted to you."

KANDI GALLATY, Author, *Disciple Her*

"*Write It on Their Hearts* is the most clear, accessible, and practical book written to help parents disciple their kids. Through this book Chris and Melissa will help you understand how to build relationships with your kids that lead to eternal impact."

BEN TRUEBLOOD, Director, Student Ministry, Lifeway Christian Resources

"*Write It on Their Hearts* isn't just a great book; it's a necessary read for every parent. In a world demanding your attention, you're reminded to chase after what matters most—what matters for eternity. A must-read for every parent who is serious about raising Jesus-loving disciples."

JERRAD LOPES, Founder, Dad Tired

"Many parents do not know how to disciple their own children. Yes, we need to invite parents into a spiritual awakening in their own lives. And we need to call them to lead and disciple their children. But the very next step must be *showing* them, in a practical way, *how* to actually do that. That is what Chris and Melissa Swain have done."

RICHARD ROSS, PHD, Senior Professor, Southwestern Baptist Theological Seminary

"In *Write It on Their Hearts*, Chris and Melissa help parents like me (a mom who feels like I have no idea what I'm doing) to navigate a tough and weighty calling. They cut through the fog of nebulous 'I shoulds' and stick to Scripture, offering ways for us to engage with our kids over the long haul. What a gift this is for parents like me, who need biblical wisdom and practical ideas."

KRISTEN WETHERELL, Author, *Humble Moms* and *Hope When It Hurts*

WRITE IT

ON THEIR

HEARTS

Chris Swain WITH **Melissa Swain**

thegoodbook
COMPANY

thegoodbook.com | thegoodbook.co.uk
thegoodbook.com.au | thegoodbook.co.nz | thegoodbook.co.in

Cover design by Faceout Studio
Art direction and design by André Parker

ISBN: 9781784987749 | Printed in India

Caedmon and Honor,
Run hard after Jesus,
no matter where it takes you.

CONTENTS

Foreword

By Robby Gallaty

Everyone who was friends with Chris knew he lived purposefully. Everything he did was intentional.

Whether it was learning a new hobby, researching a leadership-development tool, finding a new fishing lure that worked, or perfecting a card trick—all things we both loved—he was fully invested, which is why we got along so well. One responsibility he focused on more than most was discipling his family at home. Our staff would say often, "If I was half the dad Chris was...," or "I really need to do with my kids what Chris is doing with his."

Two years ago, I lamented to Chris about the lack of discipleship resources that would help parents to invest in their children. "We need someone to write about how to disciple children," I said. "We need someone to write the book who is actively practicing what he preaches." The person that came to mind was him. He disclosed, "I didn't tell you this yet, but I've been working on a manuscript outline for the past few months." I couldn't think of anyone better to provide a guidebook for discipling.

Writing can be a chore for many; however, *Write It on Their Hearts* was not for Chris. Regularly, I would walk into his office to find a new picture, diagram, or acrostic on his whiteboard. "Hey, do you have a minute for me to run this by you?" was a consistent phrase I heard. The writing process was life-giving from the start. As with everything, Chris set deadlines for himself, normally months before the actual date to provide a margin for unexpected things happening. He set a goal to finish the manuscript by July 9, 2021. Why? His words were, "Pastor, that's the day before you leave for your month sabbatical. I want to get it in your hands to read and comment on while you're away." Neither of us knew at the time how important that completion date would be.

On July 9, while both of our wives were out of town with our children, Chris and I had planned to go to a local baseball game. Just before he was to arrive at my house, I got a call that he was being rushed to the ER. We spent the next six days at the hospital day and night, praying and waiting for Chris to come out of the non-responsive state he was in. People from all over the country texted, emailed, and called to say they were praying alongside us for a healing miracle. On July 15, God answered our prayer by giving Chris the ultimate healing in heaven.

Even though he's been gone for months now, I think about him every day. I still can't comprehend why God would take my best friend prematurely. I don't know if I will ever understand it this side of eternity, but that doesn't minimize my trust in God's sovereign plan.

Even though Chris is not with us anymore, these final words will continue to impact lives for years to come. Everything Chris believed about not wasting one's life, making the most of the time we have, and leaving a legacy long after you're gone was realized on July 15, the day he went to be with Jesus. He practiced everything he presents in this book. He didn't write as an ivory-tower theologian, propped up in a monastery, secluded from the world. No, he shares from experience, as a fellow pilgrim on the journey of parenthood, figuring it out along the way.

What you have in your hands is not just a resource to read and put on a shelf. It's a manifesto Chris and his wife, Melissa, lived by. From the vantage point of someone with a front-row seat to the principles in action outlined in this book, I can attest to the impact they have made in his family and mine.

Robby Gallaty, Pastor, Long Hollow Church
December 2021

Introduction

Who Is Discipling Your Children?

What's so hard about being a parent? As a youth pastor, I asked myself this question often. I would encourage the parents of my students to raise their children well. To instill biblical principles in their lives. To bring them to every church event possible. I told parents, "You are the primary disciple-maker in your kid's life." And I believed it. I told every parent I connected with that if they just did a few simple things, they would be successful.

I remember the looks on parents' faces when I would tell them just how easy it was to lead their children to be like Jesus. These parents looked at me with exasperation, others looked incensed, and some looked at me with pity in their eyes. Every once in a while, a parent would say, "Chris, some day when you have kids, you'll understand why it's not that easy." I would just nod for that parent, but inside, I was disagreeing. It couldn't be that hard, I worked with kids all day every day, I knew how it worked. Then that "someday" arrived. My first child was born.

As I held my brand-new baby boy in my arms, I thought about the future. What if I made a mistake with him? What if I drove him to a life of disappointment or failure? What if all the things I had said and taught as a youth leader weren't enough? Could everything I believed about raising Christ-centered kids be theory alone? The faces of those parents haunted me as my heart raced. I wanted to go back in time and slap myself. The sudden realization that I knew absolutely nothing about being a parent set in. I was clueless. What was God doing putting me in charge of a living, breathing human being? If there had been a camera in the delivery room, it would have zoomed in on my face to highlight my misguided understanding of the weight of parenthood.

Since that momentous day, I have gained a greater understanding and appreciation of the challenges parents face. Raising my own children, a teenager and an elementary-aged child, has exposed me to both sides of the coin. It is definitely not easy. There is no shortcut. If we want to lead our children to Jesus and for them to be like Jesus, it will take work. But there is so much more to it than that. Ultimately, it comes down to some good news and bad news.

Let's start with the bad news. Being a parent is tough. Let that understatement sink in. You are in charge of another human. The highest of highs and lowest of lows come at you on a daily, if not hourly basis (ok, for real, minute by minute). The blessing and the agony of parenting are oars in the same boat. One minute they're melting your heart with macaroni art, the next minute they're melting your favorite plant in the firepit out back. Children don't come with a how-to manual. There is no pause button for this season of life. There is no helpline, no tech support. God blesses you with a child and entrusts that child's care and well-being to you.

Parenting is tough but add to that the difficulty of being a Christian parent in a post-Christian culture. Even the easier elements of parenting are dialed up to the highest difficulty in this day and age. Teaching your children to walk pales in comparison to teaching them to walk with wisdom in a world flooded with foolishness. Likewise, teaching your children to talk, and use proper grammar is child's play compared to teaching them to be slow to speak, and to do so with grace and humility amidst the godless banter of modern media.

This post-Christian culture is a monumental challenge, but it is nothing new. Thousands of years ago, the world's greatest ruler set out to conquer Jerusalem. He had the largest army, the greatest tactics, and all the resources he would need to accomplish the task ten times over. But instead of overwhelming the city with force, he did something very different. He came bearing sacrifices to Jehovah.

Alexander the Great used a brilliant method to conquer the culture.[1] He didn't come to destroy the societal norms and traditions; he came to celebrate them. But there was a caveat: he introduced exciting new elements to the mix. Mr. The Great was ok with whatever it is you held as important, he just wanted to share some intriguing new stuff that your people were sure to love. And by doing so, he introduced four specific means by which he ultimately integrated you into his empire.

1. Entertainment

Theater and the arts were a critical piece of Alexander's strategy. Popular culture crafted shared experiences that fostered a new mindset in the hearts of the people.

While often indirect, entertainment is most commonly a commentary on culture. The real question is, who is crafting the commentary, and what are they trying to say through it?

2. Information

In our modern world, we have access to information instantly. We can quickly access even the vaguest information within seconds on our phone or device. But in the time of Alexander the Great, things moved much slower. Couriers had to deliver messages from town to town. Often, critical information would take days or weeks to reach various cities. It isn't hard to imagine the power someone could wield if they had control over this information network. We see it in our world every day. What news channel do you trust? Whose version of the news is more accurate? We typically like our news filtered by whoever leans our way politically. But Alexander was in control of the news quite literally. Not only could he determine when people heard what was going on, he could also shape the narrative.

3. Sports

Imagine the children gathering to listen to the rabbi consistently, their free time filled with elements that engrained what it meant to be Jewish. When Alexander the Great brought sports into the culture, the focus shifted from things of eternal consequence, to the story about the fastest runner in all the known world. As an avid lover of football, it is all too easy for me to see how the insignificant pastime of sports can occupy my thoughts and lead to distraction. I'm not trying to create a feeling of guilt here, but perhaps you too can sense the ease with which things like sports can affect a culture.

4. Education

When children learned in Jerusalem, they learned of their heritage. They were taught the Torah (the first five books of the Bible) as well as important moves of God through the ages. Alexander didn't tell the people to stop teaching these things; he simply brought new information to add to the mix. What about the other gods celebrated across multiple cultures? Alexander encouraged those as well. Education shapes children's minds, that is no surprise. But when education is institutionalized, there is always a narrative framework by which educators work. We must again ask the question, who controls this narrative? Alexander knew that if he could reach children, generations to come would move farther away from their existing culture to embrace his new one.

Alexander the Great's method for assimilating cultures was so effective that he became one of history's most powerful rulers. It doesn't take a genius to look at our current post-Christian culture and realize that perhaps we too have been enveloped in a modern version of Hellenism. For parents trying to raise disciples of Jesus, we must be hyperaware of the methodology of the enemy to distract and derail us. We live in a vulture culture that has an agenda to prey upon our children. It is subversive, and it is effective. And guess what, it only gets more challenging! (Stay with me. The good news is coming!)

68% of Christians make a decision to follow Jesus before they turn 18 years old. That means the chances of your child following Jesus after they leave home decreases dramatically. Knowing this, the challenge to lead our children to follow and be like Jesus is even more critical. This is especially poignant when we look at the timeline we have with our children. Think about your children's time with you. You'll get about 6,570 days with your children before they turn 18. 5,840 days before they get their driver's license. 4,380 days before they hit the teenage years. 2,190 days before they start school. 365 days before our children learn to walk. I don't know where you are in this timeline but if it's anywhere after your child is born then you have even less time to get intentional. Look at this time chart:

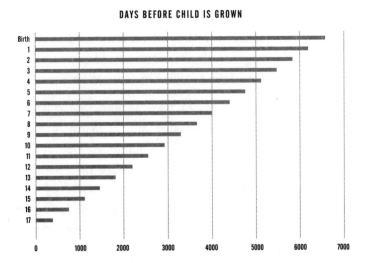

DAYS BEFORE CHILD IS GROWN

If that visual doesn't get your mind racing and your heart beating faster, then you've got it together more than most. At the time of writing this, my children are 14 and 10. Realizing I only have a few more years to impact my oldest child is mind blowing. Just yesterday it seems he was learning to ride his bike, and, in a year, he will be getting his learner's permit to drive a car! Lord, help us!

Take a moment and reflect deeply upon this time chart. Perhaps, like me, you have a teenager, and you see just how much less time you have ahead. Maybe you have a newborn, and it feels like you have all the time in the world. Over my years in ministry, parents have told me again and again, "Don't take your time for granted; it flies by!" I cannot reiterate that truth to you enough. Maybe you already understand how critical each moment is with your children. The challenge is that, in the moment, we rarely feel the pressure of losing time. It's only when we reflect back that we realize how short these years are.

When it comes to the little time we have with our children, we must strike a balance between being overbearing and ever-present, and becoming apathetic. One way to keep things in perspective is to map out the milestones in our children's lives. This way we can have more intentional clarity when we engage with our children. Set a reminder on your calendar to look over milestones on your horizon. Think about key moments like your child getting a phone or moving from elementary to middle school. Being more aware of these times will help you lean into them as they happen.

Parents are facing a vulture culture that uses the Hellenistic tactics of Alexander the Great. As we have seen, we are also up against a time constraint. Additionally, there is a minimization of faith in our culture. If we analyze the top child-rearing values across American adults, we find that being responsible is number one. Hard work is number two.

And coming in third at just 30% of those polled is faith.[2] I guess we could celebrate the fact that faith is even on the list, but, in this day and age, that's not saying much. Over half of adults contend that Christianity is just one of many faith options, and they are more likely to pick and choose beliefs rather than adopt those of a church or denomination.[3] So for many parents, faith is not a top priority for their children, and what faith they do have tends to be a buffet of preferential beliefs rather than foundational orthodoxy.

Let's get this straight:

- As Christian families, we are living in a vulture culture designed to integrate our children.

- We are up against a time constraint to lead our children to Christ.

- The culture's focus for our children is more about hard work than pursuing their faith.

- The majority of parents aren't modeling an orthodox faith worth following, anyway.

Yeah, like I said, let's start with the bad news. The odds seem stacked against Christian parents. It feels over-whelming. It may even seem insurmountable as you think of your own children. But don't despair and give up yet! The bad news is pretty bad, but the good news—well the good news is here to save the day.

A Person

The good news, parents, is this: we have hope. And not just any hope, but the hope of glory, Jesus Christ in us. While there are no perfect parents, there is a perfect God. Jesus provides us with a purpose and a plan. So, while the odds aren't in our favor, Jesus is the one who makes the way for us to succeed. I'll take those odds any day.

Think about this: the first children ever born were not born in the Garden of Eden. They were born after the fall. That means there have been no perfect parents. God alone is the perfect Father. Presenting your children mature in Christ is the goal. The challenges pushing back against this goal are strong, but the apostle Paul wrote in Colossians 1:29, "I labor for this, striving with his strength that works powerfully in me." Jesus Christ—working in us—can and will accomplish his will; we don't have to go it alone. We don't have to hope it all works out. We can know that Jesus is at work in us and through us to impact our children. The Holy Spirit is at work empowering us to accomplish his will.

A Purpose

Here's more good news: we have a purpose. Jesus is very clear to his disciples in Matthew 28:18-20: "Jesus came near and said to them, 'All authority has been given to me in heaven and on earth. Go, therefore, and make disciples of all nations, baptizing them in the name of the Father and of the Son and of the Holy Spirit, teaching them to observe everything I have commanded you. And remember, I am with you always, to the end of the age.'"

Our purpose as parents is clearly defined here: we are to make disciples. That includes our children. I'd argue that, for parents, our children are our priority in making disciples. The Great Commission begins in the home. This is the purpose each and every Christ-following parent must embrace. The person, Jesus Christ, gives us this purpose: to make disciples. That's good news.

We don't have to scour the internet looking for a reason.

We don't have to do any soul-searching in order to discover some deep truth.

We don't have to take an assessment to be told what our focus should be.

Jesus summed it all up in these two words: make disciples.

A Plan

The good news is we have a person in Jesus, who gives us a purpose in the Great Commission. That leads us to the last bit of good news: we have a plan. This book will walk you through the plan, but here it is in a nutshell: discipleship happens when we spend intentional time with our children. It is in these moments that God writes his word on their hearts. He does the writing, but we help create the atmosphere for this to take place. There are six key elements that Jesus modeled in his discipleship:

1. Love
2. Prayer
3. Connection
4. Scripture
5. Accountability
6. Rest

You will be able to develop a strategy that is custom-fit for your season of parenting. Remember the beginning of the chapter where I recalled my early days of youth ministry, happily telling parents how easy it was to lead their kids to follow and be like Jesus? Well, I wasn't completely wrong.

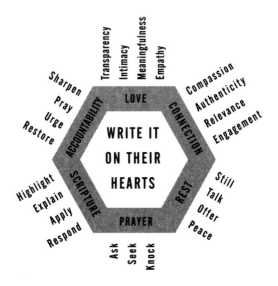

The plan is simple. What's difficult is the investment. I can show you how to get to my house on a GPS and it won't take me more than a few minutes. But the actual trip is going to take time and effort and resources. I know now that parenting is hard work. Parenting to make disciples is even more challenging. But the plan itself, it's simple. What we have to do to work the plan will take time and effort and resources. And that is anything but easy. Discipling our children will not be easy, but it will be worth it. So just what is the plan? That, we will discuss in full in the next chapter.

Take some time to think through specific ways the culture has impacted your children. List some key responses to how you want to help them navigate the four areas we discussed:

- *Entertainment:* How does your child's exposure to TV, YouTube, Twitch, and social media influence their perspective on life? How does it impact their faith?

- *Education*: What are your children being taught? What are teachers leading them to believe about society, religion, ethics, and other key subjects? Have you had discussions with them about these areas and what you believe?

- *Sports*: How do extra-curricular activities take a priority in your home? How are each of your children learning to prioritize their pursuit of Jesus over their pursuit of athletic success?

- *Information*: Where are your children learning about the events of the day? Whose version of those events are they seeing as most trusted? Have you spoken with your children about how to discern truth when everyone has their version of what is right and wrong?

In addition to examining the impact of the culture on your children, here are some more key practices to try:

- Chart out the key milestones in each of your children's lives.

- Create a reminder that you get on a consistent basis that reminds you of key dates and the time you have left with your children.

- Consider developing some values that your family can adopt as guiding principles. Write them down and talk through them. Examples might be: we tell the truth, we seek Jesus first in all circumstances, we show grace to one another, etc.

1. A Crockpot, Not a Microwave

Disciple Them Like Jesus

Movies last about two hours. If they are good, they deliver an unforgettable experience that resonates and leaves an impression. The average movie takes about two years between announcement and release. The production time involves many moving parts, from developing a script, to hiring actors, to shooting and editing the final product. During production, there are many moments the directors, actors, and crew members experience that shape the finished product. The viewers of the movie still only experience that two-hour finished product. They don't see the...

- number of takes to get each shot right
- thousands of hours of digital, lighting, and sound effects
- flubbed lines by the actors
- stunt crews shooting and reshooting for the perfect shot
- story edits and script changes
- many hours of cutting and editing the finished product.

These are just a few things that go into creating a movie. While I am no expert on making films, I can assure you that thousands of hours go into each project. Yet, viewers only experience two. And these two hours determine whether or not the film is a success. When it comes to discipling our children, we must shift our focus from the end product to the thousands of small moments it requires to lead them to who Jesus created them to be. Raising a child who follows Jesus cannot happen overnight.

I am a member of several Facebook parenting groups. I find them useful for asking questions and getting help with parenting needs. One of the most frequent questions posted on these group pages is how to help older children obey. They range from, "How do I get my 18-year-old to follow the house rules?" to "How do I get my grown children focused on spiritual things?"

While these questions are relatively broad, they are difficult to answer. These parents are looking for solutions, in the moment, to needs that are very real. The challenge is that the answers, the solutions, are not short-term quick fixes. Discipleship is not microwavable. It is a crock-pot recipe that requires time to take root and marinate.[4] What can you tell a young adult in their late teens or early twenties if they have not already been on the journey of following Jesus? Discipleship is possible at that stage, but it is far more difficult. Often, parents walking through this stage realize, too late, that the investment needed to have taken place years prior. This leaves them with guilt or regret that they have not invested as well as they could have.

Each decision we make, each opportunity we embrace or decline, results in the legacy we build. I'm not saying we can completely avoid regret, because we are all sinners and there are no perfect parents, but we can certainly curb or reduce regret if we choose to take every opportunity we have with our kids. Do you know what the opposite of regret is? It's fulfillment, satisfaction that you did what you should have done. We defeat regret when we say yes in every single day to what we know we must do. Even when we are busy. Even when there are big pressing issues that derail our plans.

Each decision we make, each opportunity we embrace or decline, results in the legacy we build.

Before you shake this notion off because you're busy and say, "Chris, you just do not know how wired my child is and how obnoxious and needy they can become and how bouncing-off-the-walls-like-a-squirrel wild they are," think about this: God, your Father in heaven, is never too busy to listen to you. He never says, "Maybe later."

He has never ignored you.

He has never minimized your pain.

He has never withheld his affection from you.

He has never regretted, even for a moment, his moments with you.

Now, I get it, he's God and you're not. Thank goodness for that, right? But he is our example of a perfect parent, a perfect Father. If we want to experience a fulfilling relationship with our children, and if we want to live without regret, we must look to the Lord and learn from him when it comes to parenting. We see the Lord do this throughout Scripture. Jeremiah 31:33 tells us:

> *Instead, this is the covenant I will make with the house of Israel after those days"—the LORD's declaration. "I will put my teaching within them and write it on their hearts. I will be their God, and they will be my people.*

Make no mistake, it is God who writes his word on the hearts of his people. But there is an environment in which we can help our children become more receptive to God's writing. Deuteronomy 6:4-9 helps us understand this more clearly:

> *Listen, Israel: The LORD our God, the LORD is one. Love the LORD your God with all your heart, with all your soul, and with all your strength. These words that I am giving you today are to be in your heart. Repeat them to your children. Talk about them when you sit in your house and when you walk along the road, when you lie down and when you get up. Bind them as a sign on your hand and let them be a symbol on your forehead. Write them on the doorposts of your house and on your city gates.*

The Bible is clear for parents that these words are to be in your heart and the process is as follows:

- Repeat them to your children
- Talk about them at home
- Talk about them when you are out of the house
- Talk about them at bedtime
- Talk about them when you wake up
- Keep the word close to you
- Post the word in your home

We provide an opportunity for God to write his word on the hearts of our children when we do these things. When we spend intentional time and have intentional conversations with them, God writes. Start a few conversations with your children like this:

- What is God doing in your life right now?
- What specific area would you like to grow in more as you follow Jesus?
- How are you living out what Jesus is teaching you today?
- What is one way you can glorify the Lord today with your life?
- How can I help you follow Jesus more this week?

These conversations help us create opportunities for God to write on our children's hearts. But our culture also wants to write on the hearts of our children. Remember Alexander the Great and his strategy to win hearts and minds? Hellenism is alive and well as it works to create the atmosphere needed for the culture to write its agenda on our children's hearts. And it won't stop.

We have to change our mindset about how God works through us as parents to accomplish his will.

We parents must be intentional with our time and how we spend it with our children. Two powerful words: intentional time. That's the secret. The beauty of this is that we don't have to formulate some new game plan to add to our already over-busy lives. We have to change our mindset about how God works through us as parents to accomplish his will. The change we need to make is clear, but that doesn't mean it's easy.

Choosing to be intentional with our children is not the easy way, but it is so worthwhile. It is the way to significant impact and Christ-centered influence. As parents, we make the most difference in our children's lives by giving them the greatest treasure we have: time. But we must choose to spend this currency rather than store it up and save it for "someday."

How Jesus Discipled

Jesus discipled his twelve disciples by intentionally investing in them over time. Don't let the simplicity of that statement undermine its weight. When the God of the universe, Lord of all creation, Giver and Sustainer of life, chooses how to disciple his people, he opts to spend intentional time. That's his method. Likewise, we parents must choose to engage intentionally with our children for spiritual investment.

As we examine Scripture, we find that Jesus did a few specific things to maximize his investment in the twelve disciples. For our purposes, I've distilled these down into a list of six facets of discipleship that work together to help parents and children to grow more like Jesus as we follow him.

LOVE. The first element of Jesus' intentional discipleship is love. Jesus makes it quite clear in Matthew 22:35-40:

> *And one of them, an expert in the law, asked a question to test him: "Teacher, which command in the law is the greatest?" He said to him, "**Love the Lord your God with all your heart, with all your soul, and with all your mind.** This is the greatest and most important command. The second is like it: **Love your neighbor as yourself.** All the Law and the Prophets depend on these two commands."*

Jesus exemplified all the commands of the Lord and lived a perfect life. So, we know that he loved God with all of his heart, and he loved his neighbor as himself. Not only can we trust that Jesus emulated this kind of love because the Scriptures commanded it, but also because he literally gave his life for us to be saved, the ultimate act of love. An effective discipling parent will operate out of this biblical love for their children. We will discover how to be intentional with love by spending *TIME* with our children. This simple acronym will help us know, remember, and put into action *Transparency, Intimacy, Meaningfulness,* and *Empathy.*

CONNECTION. Jesus modeled connection. This connection is personal with every believer and modeled by the Holy

Spirit dwelling within us. God, throughout history moved from dwelling *with* His people to dwelling *within* his people. Notice how God moves from dwelling in the tabernacle to dwelling in the temple to dwelling in the flesh through Jesus, to now dwell in us through the Holy Spirit. God has pursued us and desired a closer connection with us in each stage of his pursuit. We must emulate Jesus and pursue connection with our children. Why? Because it is through this connection that we can help our children grow and be more like Jesus.

ACCOUNTABILITY. Accountability most often feels negative. We tend to see it as pointing out what someone is doing wrong. But the real purpose is to help fellow believers in their spiritual journey. Galatians 6:1-2 says:

> *Brothers and sisters, if someone is overtaken in any*
> *wrongdoing, you who are spiritual, restore such a person*
> *with a gentle spirit, watching out for yourselves so that*
> *you also won't be tempted. Carry one another's burdens;*
> *in this way you will fulfill the law of Christ.*

Notice that your spirit is to be gentle when you hold others accountable. Additionally, we are to carry one another's burdens. It's difficult to see biblical accountability as harsh finger-pointing when we operate with a gentle spirit, bearing each other's burdens.

PRAYER. Prayer is communication with the Lord. It is how Jesus communicated with the Father. The disciples asked Jesus to teach them how to do only one thing in all of Scripture: how to pray. Jesus gave his disciples a model for prayer in Luke 11:1-4:

He was praying in a certain place, and when he finished,
one of his disciples said to him, "Lord, teach us to pray,
just as John also taught his disciples."
He said to them, "Whenever you pray, say,
Father,
your name be honored as holy.
Your kingdom come.
Give us each day our daily bread.
And forgive us our sins,
for we ourselves also forgive everyone
in debt to us.
And do not bring us into temptation."

Jesus had already shared this model prayer on the Sermon on the Mount in Matthew 6, but here he reiterates it for the disciples. The key to praying is centered on the phrase, "Your kingdom come." This is the pivotal point we must teach our children. Praying is asking God to bring his kingdom. We know we are praying the way Jesus modeled when we focus on his kingdom. Jesus provides the model prayer and then he does something he would often do with the disciples; he explains it further. In this explanation and application, Jesus tells them to ask, seek, and knock. These three words will help us model and teach our children to pray.

SCRIPTURE. Scripture is the foundation of our faith. God's word plays an integral role in every disciple's life. I simply cannot overstate how critical the word is in growing our children to be like Jesus. Let's reflect on just a few of the claims the Bible makes about itself:

2 Timothy 3:16-17 says, *"All Scripture is inspired by God and is profitable for teaching, for rebuking, for correcting, for training in righteousness, so that the man of God may be complete, equipped for every good work."*

Isaiah 40:8 says, *"The grass withers, the flowers fade, but the word of our God remains forever."*

Hebrews 4:12 says, *"For the word of God is living and effective and sharper than any double-edged sword, penetrating as far as the separation of soul and spirit, joints and marrow. It is able to judge the thoughts and intentions of the heart."*

Psalm 119:105 says, *"Your word is a lamp for my feet and a light on my path."*

Beyond these key passages about the word of God, remember that the Word became flesh and dwelt among us in Jesus Christ. No one can follow Jesus and reject the word. We need to learn to help our children engage with the word of God. Disciples of Jesus need to do more than acquire knowledge about the Bible, we need to apply what it says to our daily lives.

No one can follow Jesus and reject the word.

REST. Rest is vitally important in our culture of hurry. Half of all fathers claim their family time suffers from a hurried lifestyle and 40% of mothers feel the same way.[5] We serve a God who has commanded us to rest, and who demonstrated rest for us. The Sabbath is probably the most ignored commandment in our culture today by well-meaning Christ-followers. But God is clear about engaging in rhythms of rest:

God rested in Genesis 2:1-3: *"So the heavens and the earth and everything in them were completed. On the seventh day God had completed his work that he had done, and he rested on the seventh day from all his work that he had done. God blessed the seventh day and declared it holy, for on it he rested from all his work of creation."*

God commanded his people to rest in Exodus 20:8-10: *"Remember the Sabbath day, to keep it holy: You are to labor six days and do all your work, but the seventh day is a Sabbath to the LORD your God."*

Jesus provides rest for our souls in Matthew 11:28-30: *"Come to me, all of you who are weary and burdened, and I will give you rest. Take up my yoke and learn from me, because I am lowly and humble in heart, and you will find rest for your souls. For my yoke is easy and my burden is light."*

Jesus is the Lord of the Sabbath in Matthew 12:8: *"For the Son of Man is Lord of the Sabbath."*

Jesus is our Sabbath rest in Hebrews 4:9-11: *"Therefore, a Sabbath rest remains for God's people. For the person who has entered his rest has rested from his own works, just as God did from his. Let us, then, make every effort to enter that rest, so that no one will fall into the same pattern of disobedience."*

While Scripture is clear about the Sabbath and our need for rest, our culture runs counter to the very idea. We want to do and do and do and we want something to do while we wait on what we will do next. A healthy disciple develops healthy rhythms of rest and we will help our children develop this practice.

Putting It All Together

If you are like my wife, Melissa, you are already thinking of ways to map out these six elements and schedule when and how you will implement each one. If you are more like me, you pick one and jump into the week with a very loose idea of how you will work on that with your child. My wife is a planner, I'm more of a by-the-seat-of-my-pants kind of organizer. The good news is, the structure of this book will work equally well for the planner and the pantser. At the end of the book, you'll find the Family Discipleship Plan, which will allow you to plan as extensively or as minimally as you'd like. No matter how you operate, remember that the goal is to be intentional with your time as you invest in your children.

> **You will never regret the time and effort you put into investing in your child's spiritual growth.**

I will be honest, discipling your children will not be easy. It may even be one of the most difficult things you do. But I promise you this: you will never regret the time and effort you put into investing in your child's spiritual growth. I am coming to you as a fellow parent asking you to take this leap with me. You can do it!

Write It on Their Hearts

- Pray, asking God to give you clarity on where to begin with your child.

- Determine which of these six elements you are most in need of growing personally. Think or journal through your thoughts on why that may be so.

- Determine which element is most needed for your child right now and choose to start there in your discipleship journey.

- Reflect on your personal discipleship journey. What areas were most impactful for you? What conversations or milestones do you feel are critical to share with your child?

- What are some regrets you have about how you have led your child spiritually? Pray and release those past failings to the Lord. If God has given you a new day, you have access to a new start. Identify the regrets and get intentional about how you can avoid them going forward as you embrace discipling your children.

- Slow down and rest in the fact that it will be a long process. No matter how old your children are, disciples are made in a lifetime, not a day.

- Spend time asking the Lord to help you know the next step to take as you lead your child to be like Jesus.

2. Tea Parties, Jiu Jitsu, and the Most Important Thing

Show Them You Love Them

"Love your children—and let them know you love them. Children who experience love find it far easier to believe God loves them." – Billy Graham

Hearing your child cry evokes so many emotions. You feel frustration as your child cries through a temper tantrum. You feel bittersweet joy as they shed tears at their wedding.

The tears of my son sparked surprising emotions from me one afternoon. We had parked in our garage and were heading into the house. Caedmon, my son, was four then and had been told many times not to run in the garage. The previous owners of the house had painted the garage floor and the paint combined with the water that dripped from our vehicles made the floor slippery. I heard Caedmon's feet smacking the concrete as he rushed around the car. I watched helplessly when he hit a slick spot. His feet went flying and he slammed into the garage floor.

The tears were instant. I rushed over and picked up my son and held him close. I could have been mad; he had disobeyed. I could have been frustrated that someone thought it would be smart to paint a concrete garage floor. I could have felt smug since I'd warned Caedmon of this very outcome. But I didn't feel any of those emotions at that moment. I simply felt the love I had for my son. Love overshadowed my desire to punish him or even say, "I told you so."

The surprising emotions of that moment came from my realization that this is how Jesus loves me. Although I disobey, although I choose rebellion, Jesus loves me. And caught up in that moment, realizing how much Jesus loves me through my brokenness, I remembered his simple and clear command that we should love one another. In discipling our children, we must start with love, rely on the Father's love, and let love rule the process. Love is integral to effective biblical discipleship.

In discipling our children, we must start with love, rely on the Father's love, and let love rule the process.

While the above scenario was a rare moment when I got it right, the truth is I often get it wrong. As my children get older, it gets easier to respond less with love first. Shouldn't a teenager act more mature than a toddler? For sure, but that doesn't mean my response shouldn't come from a place of love. Don't get me wrong, I'm not advocating for allowing kids to run wild (we will discuss that more later). I'm saying we need to remember that as our kids grow older, love must continue to rule our responses. This is how they will learn to love others and—someday—their own children. Writing love on the hearts of our children begins with being a loving parent.

As with each of the six elements we will discuss in discipling children (see the outline in the introduction), our walk must match our talk. Before we can instill any truth or biblical principle, we must ensure we are acting out of love. We must model love for our children if we want them to understand and practice loving God and others. Let's look at two specific ways we can show love to our children and help them grow in love for God and others.

Transparency

Time leads to transparency. The time we spend with our children today equals transparency tomorrow. When children spend more time with a parent, they talk more. The familiar presence of a father or mother is foundational for open communication. The opposite is also true, in that the less time you spend together, the less you'll talk. Less conversation means less transparency. To build more open and transparent dialogue with your children, spend time with them.

John 15:15 provides insight on the power of transparency:

> *I do not call you servants anymore, because a servant doesn't know what his master is doing. I have called you friends, because I have made known to you everything I have heard from my Father.*

Jesus shared a meal with the disciples the evening before his death. In this moment he clarified their relationship. He had been transparent with them by making known everything he had heard from the Father. Remember, this is God in the flesh. He had every right to withhold information, but he chose to share. This transparency created a connection that moved these men from being disciples to being friends. Feel the weight of what Jesus was doing here. This is precisely how transparency as a parent grows the bond of love between you and your children. We may think that withholding information will be helpful, we want to protect our kids from the realities of life. But Jesus shows us that it is through transparency that we become friends.

The more transparent we are with our children, the more opportunity we have to grow in love for one another.

When my daughter was younger, she enjoyed setting up tea parties with her stuffed animals. She would occasionally invite me to the festivities. While it was a struggle to squeeze into the tiny furniture designed for stuffed animals and small children, I attended as many as possible. During these parties my daughter would open up and tell me all kinds of things. How her day was going. Her favorite stuffed animal. Which friend was being nice and which was being a "meany." This allowed me to share in return. I told her about my day—what I was struggling with, and how I was feeling. Admittedly, the nature of a child's tea party is light, we didn't get too deep. But this is just one example of how time spent translates into transparency. It isn't always easy, or even possible, but saying yes to these kinds of invitations from our children provides an avenue to be transparent.

Transparency is opening up to someone, letting them see the real you. It means being honest and sharing even the stuff we don't want most people to know. It means telling them the truth, even when it hurts. This is so important for your children because the old adage is true: children do what we do, not what we say. The more transparent we are with our children, the more opportunity we have to grow in love for one another.

Intimacy

As we spend time with our children, our relationship deepens. This relational depth results in the child being known by the parent and vice versa. The power of intimacy cannot be overstated in the discipling relationship. Transparency allows for parent and child to know more about one another. Intimacy is "marked by a warm friendship developing through long association."[6] Transparency is making known, intimacy grows from that knowledge. 1 Corinthians 8:3 says,

> But if anyone loves God, he is known by him.

What a powerful statement from Scripture. God knows us. This is what defines us as followers of Jesus, that we are known by God. Our identity is not based on who we know, but in who knows us.

My mother often drove me to school when I was a child. These trips were spent in silence at times, but more often we talked. Our conversations began fairly surface level, but over time they deepened. What started as transparency grew into intimacy as she began to know me, and I began to know her. There is no guarantee your conversations will go deep. But putting you and your child in an environment for greater intimacy increases the odds exponentially. Take the opportunity to get involved in the morning drive to school. If your schedule includes driving your children to school or sports practice or activities at church, these are a perfect opportunity to spend time together. The key is to be intentional with this time. Don't focus on forcing lengthy discussions about deep theology. It is the natural, everyday conversations that spark intimacy. Deeper conversations will come over time. Don't waste the time you spend with your child in the car; instead use it to be intentional with your conversations.

Another practical way to foster intimacy with your child is to join them for lunch. Take the opportunity to eat lunch with your children at school as your schedule allows. This practice shows your children that you have an interest in being together. It teaches them that you see your relationship with them as a priority. If your child's school allows, check them out and take them somewhere for lunch on occasion. This can turn a typical activity into a memorable moment your child cherishes.

Meaningfulness

Transparency and intimacy work together to build a loving relationship. This happens over time, but there are key moments we can press into to maximize the process. Every child experiences major milestones. Birthdays, graduating kindergarten, and getting a driver's license are all significant events. These are events they will remember forever. Smaller milestones are created through time spent with our children. While they are not as significant as major milestones, they are just as profound in shaping your young disciples. You and I can create an atmosphere for these smaller significant moments to take place. To do that, we must spend intentional time with our children. We often connect love with a moment. "I knew I loved her when..." "He showed me he loved me by..." The reality is these are highlight points in an ongoing relationship. We focus on those moments even though they are the capstones of the underlying relational journey. With that knowledge, we need to be laser focused on maximizing meaningful moments.

We need to be laser focused on maximizing meaningful moments.

One simple way to create meaningful moments is to read the Bible together. Not only are you helping your child develop a powerful habit, you are also connecting with them around God's word. If your children are younger, reading to them will help them experience this time with you. Even when it seems like it's no big deal, keep in mind that these small moments will be remembered and cherished by your children throughout their lives.

Another way to create meaningful moments is to think intentionally about ways you can spend time with your family. Think small! Vacations and family trips are terrific for spending time together, but they are often rare due to costs and schedules. Plan to get donuts on Saturdays. Plan a walk around your neighborhood. Plan a game night. Plan to watch a TV show together. You don't have to get super creative here. Simplicity and keeping it small-scale will make these moments happen more often.

I began taking my kids to get donuts on Saturday mornings when they were very young. While my waistline didn't benefit from this practice, our relationship certainly did. As they've gotten older and more focused on sleeping in, we've stayed home more often. But they still ask to go get donuts from time to time and recall the moments we shared. Think of some simple ways you can create meaningful moments by spending time with your kids.

Creating a culture of small but meaningful moments in your home can help ground your children in a family mindset versus a mindset focused outside the home. Outside activities aren't bad, but will never have the eternal impact on your family that meaningful moments can help facilitate. When they find meaningfulness at home, the Hellenistic culture of the world doesn't have the same temptation and pull.

Empathy

The more you know your children, the more you understand their quirks and challenges. This knowledge comes from time spent together. This is reciprocal as children learn to empathize more with their parents as they spend time with them. Empathy is a powerful emotion that builds understanding. Transparency is opening up and being honest and real with one another. Empathy is understanding the feelings, thoughts, and experiences of your children even when they don't communicate them. Once again, time is the key. Empathy grows as you spend intentional time knowing them (intimacy).

The more you and your children learn to empathize, the more profound your discipleship experience will be. When I want to have a specific conversation with one of my children, I'll take them to their choice of restaurant. There is just something about sharing a meal that helps conversation flow. I recall clearly a conversation at Chick-fil-A in which my son told me that while he enjoyed training in Brazilian Jiu Jitsu, he didn't really care about competing at tournaments. As a dad, I enjoyed watching him compete. I had to set aside my feelings about it and embrace his. I shared with him how I had faced a similar scenario as a teenager. I knew how he felt and made sure he knew that. Intentional time with our children helps us become more empathetic toward one another.

The more you and your children learn to empathize, the more profound your discipleship experience will be.

There are few things more impactful than spending dinner time together as a family. Sharing a meal together is not only a simple way to be consistent with your plan to spend time, it's also biblical. Acts 2:42 illustrates how sharing a meal was part of the early church's rhythm. Sitting down with your children for a meal creates opportunities. You can discuss the day, share stories, and simply be present with one another. The greatest challenge with this practice today is encroaching digital distraction. Make the dinner table a place where phones are unwelcome if you want greater connection. Likewise, be intentional to get conversation going. There will be some shared meals that don't feel like much helpful family interaction has taken place. But there will be those that do help grow your relationship and increase your empathy toward one another.

The time spent prioritizing your children will not go unnoticed.

One of the ways our empathy increases toward our children is when we are present at their stuff. If your children have an extra-curricular activity, try to be present as often as possible. When the years pass and your kids are grown, you will not regret this investment. I get it, soccer bores me to tears and dance recitals cause me slightly less pain than a visit to the dentist. But remember, you aren't there for the activity, you are there for your child. When you are in their world, it becomes easier to understand their minds. You gain a greater understanding as to why they are frustrated, tired, sad, happy, or excited. The time spent prioritizing your children will not go unnoticed. I have heard many adults reflect fondly about the impact of having a parent present in these moments. Determine now that you will be that kind of parent.

Transparency, Intimacy, Meaningfulness, and *Empathy* spell *TIME.* This acronym is a simple tool to help remember how to write love on your children's hearts.

Each of these things can grow when love is at the core. Discipling your children should always blossom out from this loving relationship. Jesus gave a command to love one another; he did not suggest it as an option. When we do embrace this key aspect of the discipleship process, we will be ready and able to take on this great calling no matter how difficult it gets. And it will be difficult. But it will also be the most important thing you do as a parent.

In Matthew 28:16-20 we find Jesus gathered with his disciples:

> *The eleven disciples traveled to Galilee, to the mountain where Jesus had directed them. When they saw him, they worshiped, but some doubted. Jesus came near and said to them, "All authority has been given to me in heaven and on earth. Go, therefore, and make disciples of all nations, baptizing them in the name of the Father and of the Son and of the Holy Spirit, teaching them to observe everything I have commanded you. And remember, I am with you always, to the end of the age."*

Notice the second half of verse 17: "But some doubted." The disciples weren't doubting that it was Jesus. They had already encountered him after the resurrection twice. No, they were doubting what came next: the unknown future without their Savior and friend, Jesus, walking beside them in the flesh. Jesus comforted them with the fact that he had all authority. He then gave them their mission. Finally, he told them some of the most encouraging words anyone can ever hear: "Remember, I am with you always, to the end of the age."

Discipling your children will be one of the greatest challenges you ever embrace.

Discipling your children will be one of the greatest challenges you ever embrace. But remember, Jesus is with you always. Let this truth resonate within your soul as you embark on the journey to lead your children to follow and be like Christ.

Write It on Their Hearts

- Identify ways your parents showed you love growing up. Alternately, what are some actions or attitudes you felt were unloving? Determine which of these have an impact on how you show love to your children.

- Have a conversation with your child about when they feel loved. Ask them how you can be more loving with them. (Spoiler alert: teenagers may blow this conversation off or shut down and go into silent mode. Push through and work to get some insight from them.)

- For younger children ask: How are you feeling today? What makes you happy? What makes you sad?

- Hug your children daily. It may start out awkward, but it will become natural over time.

- Tell your children you love them. Say the words out loud to them on a consistent basis. Again, if this hasn't been a habit in your family, it may feel awkward at first, but over time it becomes easier.

- Determine if there are some areas in your life where you are not being transparent with your children. Do they see you struggle with sin? How can you more transparent with your children?

- Give your children permission to ask you honest questions about your life and your walk with God. Help them see the value of open honesty.

- Lean into discovering more about your child and their interests. Pick a game, brand, show, or pastime they enjoy and let them share it with you.

- Admit to your children when you get it wrong. Apologize to them when you blow it.

- Make a game plan for how you can be more empathetic with your child. This means hearing their perspective and laying yours aside while you listen. Identify areas where you may need to show more empathy and take the necessary action.

3. It's Time for the Talk...

Teach Them to Pray

My son Caedmon and I were two hours into a three-hour drive. I was as nervous as I'd been in years because I still hadn't given him the talk. The talk was one of the main reasons we were on this journey and I had not built up the courage to start the conversation. We'd been planning the trip for a few years. A father and son, milestone, memory-making journey to the Grand Canyon. Caedmon had just turned ten and he had picked the destination. I planned to give him four things:

1. A special journal to write down notes from this trip and other important notes for life.

2. A high-quality pocket knife.

3. My full attention.

4. The talk.

I tried to get into the conversation once again after numerous false starts. We only had one hour remaining until we were at the airport. I turned down the music and looked at him through the rearview mirror. He was smiling, wearing a baseball cap, and flipping through a book he'd purchased at the canyon. "Caedmon," I stammered. He looked up from the book right into the mirror. Right into my eyes. Waiting for me to continue.

"Son, I need to tell you something important," I gulped, nerves building into a tsunami in my gut. He just stared back, completely unaware of the information I was about to drop. I felt like a doctor delivering devastating news to a patient. "Son," I said, "I don't always act the way I want to. I get angry and take that out on you and I shouldn't do that."

Wait a second. You probably thought I was talking about another talk. The Talk. The birds and the bees and all that. No, thankfully we had already done that prior to this trip. No, this was a talk I needed to have with my son in which I needed to clear the air. Clarify my heart to him. Ask him to understand me. Ask him to forgive me.

For the next hour, I talked; he listened. While he didn't say much, Caedmon did affirm what I was saying. He asked a few questions. He nodded as he listened, letting me know that he heard what I was saying. I really wished I could get him to speak to me more. I wanted him to know that we needed to dialogue in order to grow as father and son. I wish I could say that he opened up and we engaged in a deep conversation together. But he didn't, so we didn't. I was left with a desire for my son to talk to me, to speak, to open up and for our relationship to grow. That didn't happen and I couldn't really blame him; he was only ten years old. The Lord reminded me in this moment that he had that same yearning for me to speak to him. I realized that what my son was unknowingly doing was what I, as a follower of Jesus for 24 years, still did to my Father in heaven. God wants us to talk to him, to seek him in prayer. Once again, God used a moment where I had planned to teach my child to teach me as well.

Prayer isn't something we do for God; it is something that we do to be with God.

One of the greatest challenges of prayer is that we allow it to become a repetitive action we "do" for God. Prayer isn't something we do for God; it is something that we do to be with God. Much like my conversation with Caedmon, I intended it for his good, but it was really for my good. E.M. Bounds said it best, "God can move mountains and prayer moves God." It is imperative for us to teach our children to pray. There is no greater practice we can commit to that will impact our children more than to help them be on their faces seeking and pleading with God. If we desire to see change in our children, we should see prayer as the first option, not the last effort.

Teach them HOW to pray, not WHAT to pray

You want your children to be able to pray for more than a blessed meal or a good night's sleep. There is a good chance that if you ask your child to pray, they will sound very similar to you. This makes sense because they probably learned to pray by listening to your example. This is fine until we determine that their prayer is simply a rehash of ours rather than a fresh conversation with the Father.

Now, let's get real here, our own prayer may be a rehash of the person we learned to pray from ourselves. Think about how you pray for dinner with your children. Is it the same basic statement every time? Mine often is. How about when you pray for them at bedtime? Do you recite the same basic pattern each night? I often do. What's refreshing is when our children pray outside the lines that we have provided. My daughter prayed these words when she was four: "Jesus, I hope I get to have hair dye that turns all of my hair blue." While I did chuckle at the request, I couldn't help but note the sincerity of it. She was talking to God, not just regurgitating the standard "bless this food" mantra.

If we want to help our children develop an effective practice of prayer, we should teach them how, not what to pray.

We must also resist the temptation to make prayer an exchange of information or rapid-fire request line. Our culture is addicted to instant information, and we must not let prayer become like a one-way news channel that only spouts an informational narrative without pausing to listen and look for God's response. We'll talk about this more in chapter 7.

Jesus gives us the greatest example of how to teach others to pray. In Matthew 6:9 Jesus says, "Therefore, you should pray like this…" Notice that Jesus doesn't say, "Therefore, you should pray this." No, he says, "Pray like this." This is a critical difference. Jesus is illustrating that having a pattern for prayer is more important than having a memorized script. If we want to help our children develop an effective practice of prayer, we should teach them *how*, not *what* to pray. Let's take a look at the specifics of the Lord's Prayer and how it can help us teach our children.

GOD, OUR FATHER. "Our Father in heaven, your name be honored as holy." Our prayer should start with a recognition of who God is, our heavenly Father. This recognition also expands to his holiness. Beginning prayer in this way sets the foundation for anything we pray afterward. Practically, teach your children that while we have access to God who is our Father, we also should show reverence to his name and position.

God is holy and we are to honor him. This can be as simple as ensuring that you are specific about calling God either Father, Jesus, or Lord in your prayers with intentionality. Praying to "God," while accurate, is not as specific or focused on his name and position. Again, there is nothing wrong in general with this, but we can help our children and their theological understanding early if we pay closer attention to these specifics.

GOD'S AGENDA. "Your kingdom come. Your will be done on earth as it is in heaven." After beginning with the recognition of our Holy Father, we prioritize his agenda over our own. Even though we may ask God to do things in and through us, we understand that his will being done is more important than our personal desires. God is at work bringing his kingdom to earth, pursuing his will in and through his people.

My daughter once prayed asking God to "change Mama's mind about the sheet fort having to be torn down." My wife and I laughed at the focus of the prayer, and it was certainly genuine, but it was not driven by God's agenda as much as her own. I want to be careful here not to give the impression that we should not pray and ask God for specific requests in our lives. I simply want to illustrate that we should have God's agenda first and foremost on our hearts when we pray. An example of how to do this is to simply ask your children how their request connects with God's plan. Younger children will struggle with this more, but as they grow, they will begin to see more clearly how his agenda is the foundation of our prayer focus.

GOD'S PROVISION. "Give us today our daily bread." After first recognizing our holy Father, then prioritizing his will, we now move to praying for a specific need we might have. We should never be concerned that we are asking too much of God. Jesus desires for us to approach him in prayer. And if we are seeking his will in our asking, then we can be confident in our prayers. This is the area where our prayers tend to focus more on our needs. As Jesus illustrates, there is nothing wrong with this and it is even encouraged as part of his model prayer. We need to help our children know that going to the Lord in prayer is a first priority. The best way we can do this is by modeling it for them.

When struggles and difficulties hit our lives, is prayer our first response? Next time you get a call about someone struggling, stop right then and pray for them. When you drop your kids off at school, pray in the car before they leave. When great things happen, stop right then and pray, thanking God for his blessings. Let your children see you modeling this and involve them in the process when they are present. Remember, they will emulate you first and foremost in their spiritual lives. Yikes! I know, right! This can be a challenging thought, but the way forward is to determine how you want them to pursue Jesus, and model that for them.

We should never be concerned that we are asking too much of God.

GOD'S FORGIVENESS. "And forgive us our debts, as we also have forgiven our debtors." Next, we get intentional about asking the Lord to forgive our sin. Repentance is a crucial part of our relationship with Jesus. If you are like me, you may think that beginning your prayer by asking for forgiveness is more appropriate. While there is nothing wrong with that, I find it interesting that Jesus places it after asking for provision.

Perhaps he is illustrating the fact that those who follow him have been forgiven and nothing can separate us from him. Asking for forgiveness is clearly important, but by positioning it later in the prayer, Jesus is reminding us of the grace he offers us. Likewise, we should take note and not give provision to our own children as a result of their righteousness but rather their status as our own.

Of course, that doesn't mean we can't reward and encourage our children with privileges and gifts. We do it by clarifying that while there are consequences and rewards for certain actions, our role as their parent is the primary reason we provide for their needs. Their position as our children will never change and our love and provision for their needs comes with that position.

GOD'S DELIVERANCE. "And do not bring us into temptation, but deliver us from the evil one." Finally, our pattern for prayer ends by asking the Lord to deliver us from temptation and our enemy. Jesus knows that we will constantly battle our sin. He also knows that our primary weapon in this battle is prayer. By concluding our prayer with a focus on reliance upon the Lord for spiritual victory, we are reminded of this critical truth.

> **Jesus knows that we will constantly battle our sin. He also knows that our primary weapon in this battle is prayer.**

Children can ask for God's protection as they pray to be equipped with the armor of God. Ephesians 6:13-18 provides a breakdown of the full armor:

- The belt of truth
- The chest-piece of righteousness
- The sandals of readiness for the gospel
- The shield of faith
- The helmet of salvation
- The sword of the Spirit

Each of these pieces of armor speaks to a specific area of our spiritual lives. You can teach your child to use this simple method of asking God to equip them with his armor. This is a great way for younger children to engage in prayer but can also develop into a life-long prayer practice.

ASK

Now that we have broken down the Lord's Prayer, we have a clear understanding of each component. Don't let all of the ins and outs of the prayer concern you as you teach your children to pray. The *ASK* tool will help you make it memorable and simple for them. *ASK* stands for *Ask, Seek,* and *Knock*. In Luke 11:9-10 we see Jesus concluding his teaching on how to pray by explaining...

> *So I say to you, ask and it will be given to you. Seek and you will find. Knock, and the door will be opened to you. For everyone who asks receives; and the one who seeks finds; and to the one who knocks, the door will be opened.*

Jesus is teaching us that we must be persistent in our prayer. These three simple commands: ask, seek, and knock clarify that prayer is not a passive, one-sided conversation. Prayer is an active, ongoing dialogue that leads to action.

A IS FOR ASK. Asking is something we do with our mouth. We verbalize the need, the desire, or the situation to God. If our prayer coincides with God's agenda (remember his kingdom come), then the Bible says it will be given to you. So, we ask and keep asking for God to answer this prayer.

S IS FOR SEEK. Seeking is something we do with our eyes. Empowered by the Holy Spirit through the lens of God's word, we search for God at work. We seek, looking and observing for the answers to our prayer. We seek and keep seeking until God reveals his response to our prayer. We may still be asking as we seek, but we continue in this process believing he will answer as he promises to in his word.

K IS FOR KNOCK. Knocking is something we do with our hands. After we ask, we seek. Once we seek, we begin to knock on the doors that God reveals to us through the seeking. This is the part where we are stepping out in faith in response to God's work. We knock and keep knocking until the door is opened. This persistence is our faith in action. We are trusting God with the results and stepping into what he has for us. God always answers our prayers. When teaching our children to pray we must help them understand how God answers. Sometimes the answer is clear and direct, and precisely the outcome we asked for. Recently, we had a very sick relative who was not doing well. I took a call from the doctor. He said it was a very serious issue that is often fatal and that I should travel immediately to be with him. We gathered as a family and prayed for God to intervene and heal the relative. After a couple of intense weeks, God answered our prayer and the relative is back to life as normal. This is a celebration of answered prayer. I made sure the kids knew that God answered our prayer and that we should thank him for it.

Sometimes, the answer is not the answer we want. We must help our children see that sometimes, God answers differently than we want him to. He may not provide the outcome we desire, or he may allow the opposite of what we ask. We see in Scripture that the Father even responds in a way Jesus did not want. In Matthew 26:39 Jesus is asking the Father to "let this cup pass," meaning he was pleading with the Father for another available option. But the Lord did not take away the cup. Jesus teaches us in this passage that even if the outcome is not what we want, we can trust that God's will is perfect, and his ways are best. We may not understand it. We may not like it. And we may never fully get over it until we are with Jesus in glory. But until then we can trust that his will is best.

Let us spend more time praying with our kids than we do explaining the process of prayer.

Prayer is such an important spiritual discipline. Guiding our children to pray and seek the Lord is crucial. Let us be parents who engage in prayer *for* them and *with* them. Teaching children to pray happens mostly by example. Let us spend more time praying with our kids than we do explaining the process of prayer. Use the *ASK* tool to help them build a simple prayer process they can use the rest of their lives as they grow in their relationship with the Lord.

Sample Prayers

Remember, these are merely suggestions for you to adapt and use to teach your children to pray. As they are younger, keep prayer simple with relatable language. As your children get older, help them grow in their communication with the Lord.

"Father, thank you for loving me. Help me to love you with my whole heart, soul, and mind. Help me to love other people the way you love me. Amen."

"Lord, help me make choices today based on what you teach me. Show me what is right and give me the strength and courage to obey you."

"Jesus, thank you for forgiving me for my sin. Help me forgive others the way you forgive me."

"Lord, wrap me in the belt of your truth today, put on me the chest-piece of righteousness, equip my feet with readiness to share the gospel, give me the shield of faith, the helmet of righteousness, and the sword of the Spirit so I may be ready to do your will today. Amen."

Write It on Their Hearts

- Pray when your children and their needs come to mind.

- Consider journaling your prayer requests.

- Find prayer moments throughout day-to-day life. If you or your child is frustrated or struggling, stop and pray. If you are experiencing something great or achieve something awesome, stop and pray.

- Pray for your children to have relational influence with people so that God may use them to further the gospel.

- Write Luke 2:52 somewhere you can see it on an index card or as a wallpaper on your phone. Add a reminder in your phone to think about it daily. Pray it over your children as you are reminded of the passage.

- Focus on teaching your children how to pray, not specifically what to pray. While you may use a guideline to start, help them move from saying the same phrases and words to expanding their prayers beyond rote memorization.

- Short prayers are less intimidating. Show children that most prayers in the Bible were short and that they do not need to pray for a specific length of time for their prayer to be meaningful.

- When you are asked to pray for someone or something, say, "Let's pray right now." And pray for that person or need. Involve your children, let them see you actively praying as often as possible.

4. Somedays Never Come

Connect with Them

I will never forget a trip my son Caedmon and I took to go sledding. It had snowed a couple of feet deep and Caedmon loved the snow. Sleds were sold out around town, so we had purchased a small cement-mixing tub from a local hardware store. It was just big enough for me to squeeze into and let Caedmon sit in my lap. We both hugged Mama and headed out to the nearest hill. Caedmon was only three years old and looked like something out of *A Christmas Story*, barely able to put his arms down. Mama—who never stressed about being too careful with him—had indeed dressed him for the cold. We grabbed our makeshift sled and trudged through the snow to the crest of a hill.

I remember stopping as we stood on top of the hill, sled in one hand and son's gloved fingers tightly in the other, thinking, "This is one of those moments. I need to drink this in." Time froze as I reflected. Caedmon, cocooned in his blue snow clothes. The fat flakes of snow drifting lazily to the earth. The sense of excitement and joy that awaited a father and son about to sled down a hill. The smell was crisp and cool, the trees were leafless but beautiful, and the hill was still untouched. I placed the "sled" into the freshly fallen snow, sat cross-legged inside, and pulled Caedmon into my lap. And then I just sat there. How long could I sustain this moment? How long could I stretch time to retain this memory? Eventually, Caedmon's voice reminded me that we weren't moving. "Dad?"

I gave him a squeeze and said, "Ready?"

I barely heard his reply as we sped through the snow, zipping down the hill, flipping over when we hit the bottom. Our crash was a result of the inadequate cement mixer being unable to handle real sled duties, but it didn't keep Caedmon from shouting a word he has repeated many times in his life to this point and they were words I couldn't agree with more, then or now: "Again!"

It's been a decade since our sledding adventure, but I can remember it as clearly as ever. Caedmon and I have that shared experience. Shared experiences build connection and relational capitol. When I think of that time together with my son, I feel like it was a major connection. But the reality is, *he doesn't remember it at all.* That's right, this moment in time that is so powerful for me as a parent isn't even residing in my son's memory bank.

One of the greatest mistakes we make as parents is that we confuse connecting with a *moment* and connecting with our *child.* Moments are incredible, and they can be the tracks upon which connection runs, but connection is so much more than a space in time. We should strive to create moments but be wary that we aren't exchanging moments with connection. A powerful shared moment is certainly the environment in which we connect, but it isn't the connection itself. Let's take a look at how Jesus connected and see if we can emulate that with our children.

One of the greatest mistakes we make as parents is that we confuse connecting with a *moment* and connecting with our child.

Jesus Cared

Jesus built connection because he cared for people. Rather than settling for moments, he chose to invest and be present with others.

Allow that to sink in for a moment.

Throughout the Scriptures, we see him showing his love for others through compassion toward them in their struggles. Jesus was authentic; he never put on a show to impress or pretend he was anything other than who he was. Jesus did not have an air about himself, he was humble, but he was also sure.

In addition to compassion and authenticity, Jesus was always relevant. He applied truth to all situations within the context of the need or challenge. He knew the circumstances and he responded accordingly. And finally, Jesus connected so well with his disciples and others because he was engaging. Jesus gave people his full attention. He gave their problems the appropriate weight, and he pressed into the needs rather than shying away from them.

These four components: *Compassion, Authenticity, Relevance,* and *Engagement,* are just what we need to help us build and sustain connection with our children.

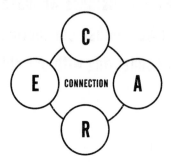

COMPASSION. Everywhere Jesus went, we see his love and compassion toward children, the sick and the masses.

- In John 8:7 Jesus shows compassion to the adulterous woman by challenging her accusers about their own sin.

- In Matthew 19:14 Jesus shows compassion to children, instructing his disciples to let the little children come to him.

- In Matthew 9 Jesus shows compassion toward the crowd because they were like sheep without a shepherd. He heals the blind, the mute, and raises the dead. Jesus frees the demon-possessed man and heals a sick woman.

Each of these acts show the heart of Jesus toward people's needs. Of course, Jesus did more than address physical needs, he showed compassion by healing our souls. There is no greater act of compassion than to live a perfect, sin-free life, and then take the punishment for the sins of the world. While we clearly can't do that for others, this incredible compassion toward us is the example he set.

Living with our children, we see the good and the bad, the highs and the lows. We show them compassion by loving them in spite of their bad days, just as Jesus loves us.

I am reminded that I need Jesus to show me compassion as a failing parent and that I should follow his example and show my children compassion.

I struggle at showing compassion to my children. For some reason, in my own brokenness, I have this mindset that my children are different than everyone else. I show my anger more quickly with them. I have higher demands on them than I do anyone else. My expectations are higher, and my compassion is simply minimal at times. I recognize this and think, *I am a terrible parent!*

It is in this kind of moment I am reminded that I need Jesus to show me compassion as a failing parent and that I should follow his example and show my children compassion. Not just *when* they don't deserve it, but *because* they don't deserve it, just as Jesus is compassionate toward me. That's the thing about compassion, it's not merit-based, it's grace-based. What great news!

Compassion operates to soften the potential barriers in your relationship with your children. By being compassionate, you are providing an opportunity for your connection to grow and flourish. The more compassion you show, the greater possibility of connection.

AUTHENTICITY. Jesus was sinless and therefore distinct from us, but he lived an authentic human life and allowed people to see this.

- In John 2:15 he tossed the temple tables in righteous indignation.

- In Luke 22:44 he asked the disciples to join him as he sweat blood and pleaded with the Father.

- In John 11:35 he wept over the loss of Lazarus.

- In Mark 4:38 he slept while the disciples were in a panic.

Whatever the situation, Jesus was real. He did not put up a front or hide any part of who he was. He showed all kinds of emotion: joy, sadness, anger, anxiety, and wonder. This kind of authenticity built a connection with those he discipled. It models for us the way we ought to disciple our children. We must be real with them. The reality is they see through our facades anyway. We should share our struggles, our fears, our challenges, and our disappointments with our kids. They will face each of these themselves and the connection they have with you as a parent will be stronger when they know you've been there too.

A friend of mine in ministry told me how he and his son had become disconnected due to a job relocation. His teenage son was not dealing with the move well because of his stage of life and the challenges that come with leaving everyone you know and replanting halfway across the country. My friend told me that his son did not speak to him for a year. A year! In an attempt to bring some healing to the relationship, John signed them up for a conference for families. The speaker challenged everyone to look directly into the eyes of their child for three minutes without speaking. My friend shared with me that within a minute he and his son had broken down and had begun to cry as they looked at each other.

Authenticity doesn't mean we tell our children everything. It means we are real about everything.

This powerful exercise broke through the barriers that had built up between father and son. It created a poignant connection through which they could grow and reconcile together. This is the kind of connection we need to have with our children, but it only happens when we are authentic with them. Authenticity doesn't mean we tell our children everything. It means we are real about everything. Authenticity as a parent means putting aside the false narrative that we are better than we really are. It means apologizing when we do wrong. It means letting our children see how real life connects with a real God. To grow connection with our children, we must be authentic.

In an age of social media when we scroll through everyone's highlight reels, authenticity can be hard to come by or even recognize. It can be shocking if we aren't expecting it. We want our children to push through this false social narrative to not only experience authenticity but live it out themselves. The best way to teach that is to model it in our own lives.

RELEVANCE. The word "relevant" has gotten a bad reputation. Relevance, as a parent, doesn't mean wearing the latest fashion or knowing the proper slang. Relevance means connecting truth into our lives and the lives of our children in a way that helps them understand and apply it. Take a look at the religious leaders of Jesus' day, the Pharisees. The Pharisees were irrelevant because they knew the truth but didn't apply it. They knew the law inside and out, but they didn't put those words into action. The Pharisees were in a position of authority with plenty of intellectual knowledge about God. Pay attention to what Jesus says about the Pharisees in Matthew 23:1-3:

> *Then Jesus spoke to the crowds and to his disciples:*
> *"The scribes and the Pharisees sit in the chair of Moses.*
> *Therefore do whatever they tell you, and observe it. But*
> *don't do what they do, because they don't practice what*
> *they teach."*

Here's the surprising insight. It is clear the Pharisees were acting in a hypocritical way, but did you notice what Jesus said in verse 3? Jesus instructs, "Do whatever they tell you." We often make the Pharisees out to be the criminals of the Gospels, but Jesus tells everyone to do what they are saying. The Pharisees were right in their knowledge of the word of God, but they were wrong in their application of the word of God. Relevance is at stake when we teach something or say something to our children, but we don't live by it ourselves.

I can list dozens and dozens of times in which my children said, "Daddy, you said don't do _____ , but you're doing it right now." I typically reply with a blank stare because I know they are right. I may even try to justify my actions for a bit. Most of the time, I reply, "You know what, you're right and I don't need to be doing that either." But not every time. And this is how the erosion of relevance happens in our homes. We teach the ideal and practice something different.

Relevance is at stake when we teach something or say something to our children, but we don't live by it ourselves.

I know you are not perfect. Neither am I, far from it. But what we must do is help our children see the tension of living for Jesus. We become more relevant by:

- apologizing when we do wrong

- agreeing that the wrong we told them not to do is also wrong for us

- acknowledging that we are in need of Jesus to live this life and that without him we can't do it.

Look at your parenting. Do you live out what you're teaching your children? Do they see you actively apply God's word in real-life situations? Are you able to have conversations with your children in which you get real with your own failings? Every single step builds relevance with them. Every single one of these actions helps them see that our faith is real and that the word is working in our lives.

Being relevant in the lives of our children builds connection. It shows them that Jesus is real to us, not just something we have knowledge about. It helps them apply and live out what we teach them, because they know it is a challenging journey. Relevance with our children means access to speak truth into their lives to which they are more likely to listen and apply.

ENGAGEMENT. Building connection with your children means engaging. There are two kinds of engagement: active and passive. Passive engagement is when something is done to you, while active engagement is, simply put, doing something. Too often we are passively engaging with our children. We are with them, but we are not present. Our heads are tilted down over our phones. Our minds are on work. Our conversations are divided between multiple people. Connection can only happen when we are actively engaging with our children.

Each week we try to have a family game night. As with any family, there are multiple personalities and preferences represented in the Swain home. I love games and could be happy playing just about anything. My daughter takes after me but being young doesn't want a game that is too complicated. My son enjoys games but has a very specific taste in the kind of game we play. It's usually the opposite of whatever my daughter chooses. My wife's favorite kind of game is called, "Can we just watch a movie instead?" Often game night slips by without anyone mentioning it because we are all trying to avoid the pre-game battle that will take place, often carrying sour attitudes into the game itself. Wasn't this designed to help us all connect and enjoy time together as a family?

Connection can only happen when we are actively engaging with our children.

Think about how Jesus engaged with people for connection. When he met a woman at a well collecting water, he could have avoided her or been too busy. After all, he was resting. Instead he engaged her in conversation, connected with her, and changed her life. When Jesus told Levi to follow him, they ended up eating dinner together. He could have just had a conversation, but he took the next step to engage. And when the disciples were sleeping in the garden, he woke them and asked them to join him in prayer. Jesus took the initiative to engage with people.

Consider scheduling a specific time and day of the week where you and your children plan to engage. This could be a movie night, lunch date, a walk, a family prayer time, or a game night. Picking your best option is the easy part. The difficult part is getting everyone to stick to the schedule. But this is where the heavy lifting of connection takes place. It is hard work to intentionally engage with your children. Even something as simple as playing a game together can create frustration. But we must work through these challenges. Connection won't happen as a result of passive engagement. Active engagement takes effort, work, prayer, and learning by both children and parents.

Somedays Never Come

By applying ourselves to *Compassion, Authenticity, Relevance,* and *Engagement*, we can identify areas to grow in for connecting with our children. Another way to help see where we might need focus is to examine the opposites of each word.

The opposite of compassion is indifference. Are there moments of indifference toward your children in your parenting? Has there been a build up of indifference toward them?

The opposite of authenticity is unreliability. Do you present expectations and then change them for your children? Do you hold them and yourself accountable for your actions and attitudes?

The opposite of relevance is irrelevance. Are you appropriately applying the truth with your children? When they struggle, do they come to you?

The opposite of engagement is disengagement. Are you walking with your kids through their ups and downs? Are you intentionally pressing in beyond just mere presence?

Think about it: You can't build connection if you are indifferent, unreliable, irrelevant, and disengaged. None of us want to be described that way. And yet, we often fall into maintenance-mode because life gets crazy, and parenting is hard. It's tough to invest in and lead our children to be like Jesus. If we are not intentional with our children, they will find the connection they need elsewhere. Our Hellenistic vulture culture is waiting to connect with our children and draw them away from the Lord and into a society that is far from the heart of God.

Often, connection with our children gets delayed in the busyness of life. We want to connect, but we are too busy with everything else. One of the most challenging elements of parenting is all of the stuff we want to say, or wish we would do, or plan to do "someday." Then we don't say it, or do it, and eventually someday is too far gone, and our kids have become adults. It's not going to be easy, but you must decide that today is the day to say the stuff, do the things, and bury the nebulous "someday" because that day is today!

You must decide that today is the day to say the stuff, do the things, and bury the nebulous "someday."

Write It on Their Hearts

- List some ways you are compassionate and some ways in which you struggle to be compassionate. Reflect and pray over this list.

- Ask your child how you can be more compassionate with them.

- Identify some ways that you consistently show the opposite of what you teach. Perhaps it's anger when you are behind the wheel, or a tone you take when you are struggling with your children. Discuss these with your family.

- Decide on and implement a phrase or word that will help you know when you are crossing this line with your children. Something like, "Mom, can we stop and think about what we are saying?"

or, "Remember, Matthew 23?" These may seem forced at first but, over time, they can be helpful to remind us and help us address our attitudes and actions in the moment.

- Have a talk with your child about the disconnect between what you say and what you do. Help them understand the journey of repentance and forgiveness as we seek to live like Jesus:

  - We sin, even after following Jesus.

  - When we choose to disobey, we ask Jesus to forgive us.

  - Jesus forgives us and teaches us to go and sin no more.

  - The Holy Spirit inside every believer helps us live like Jesus.

  - Let's help each other to live like Jesus.

- Have a discussion with your child about the things they like to do with you. Think of a few ways you can implement these moments on a consistent basis.

- Consider having a weekly game or movie night with your children. Plan it. Schedule it. And stick with it!

- Go for a walk or drive with your child. Sit on the porch and let conversation flow.

5. The Book Is Better

Teach Them to Read the Bible

My son Caedmon is an avid reader. He likes all kinds of stories, but his favorite are post-apocalyptic dystopian books targeted at young adult readers. He was reading a series recently that he fell in love with, and he devoured the books at an incredible pace. Around the time he was halfway through the books, we discovered that there were also movies for the series. Caedmon immediately asked to watch them. I had read the first book in the series myself and was also interested in how a movie might adapt the story. We popped some popcorn and started the movie with high expectations.

When the movie ended, I asked Caedmon what he thought. "It was good but nothing like the book," he began. "The ending was totally different, and they left out so much." He paused a moment, collecting his thoughts. "I liked the movie, but the book was better," he concluded.

I agreed, and when it comes to the Bible, the book is all we have, and all we'll ever need. The word of God is not just any book. All Scripture is inspired by God, or "God-breathed." The inspired word of God is "profitable for teaching, for rebuking, for correcting, for training in righteousness, so that the man of God may be complete, equipped for every good work" (2 Timothy 3:16-17). Scripture is enough.

It's 66 books composed over 1,500 years. It was written by various authors from kings to former murderers (well one of the kings was a murderer too). It is composed of letters, poetry, wisdom, prophecy, and the Gospels. The Bible is sufficient for all we need. And yet it seems we are always looking for some new insight beyond the Bible. I am tempted to buy every parenting book available. I want insight into raising my children. I want insider tips on how to get through the teenage years. I want to know how to thrive as a parent, not just survive. And so, I look and listen for everything on the subject.

We must help our children engage with God's word, not just read it.

It doesn't stop with books though; I'm also wanting another sermon, another video training, another Bible study on the topic of parenting. It doesn't stop at parenting either. I want fresh words and fresh insights in every area of my life. There's so much helpful information available, we need to ask ourselves the following questions:

- How often do I go to the word before I try other options?

- How much of my understanding of God is a result of other people's teaching rather than my own time in the word?

- What can I teach my child about God's word that isn't cut and pasted from the internet or borrowed from someone else's teaching?

- How much am I reading and applying God's word to my life?

These are tough questions that we must ask ourselves before we begin to help our children engage with God's word. Bible engagement is the most critical discipline you can have as a believer. It is most important because it impacts every other discipline in the life of a disciple. We must help our children engage with God's word, not just read it.

This is why we tend to look elsewhere for a "fresh word" or a brilliant insight, because engaging with the word is not as simple as just reading a bit daily. It means doing what it says. It means reflecting on what the Lord wants to say to you through his word, by the Holy Spirit.

So, as we determine how to lead our children into Bible engagement, let us do so by example. Let them find us reading and engaging with the word. Help them see that God's word is crucial to their lives. While we can all learn from other sources, speakers, training, and Bible studies, let's help our children understand the importance of the word of God. Show them that this book is absolutely better.

How to HEAR from God

When it comes to discipling our children by using the word of God, we want to ensure that we go beyond simple reading. We want them to engage with the word. While reading the word is certainly the starting point for engagement, it is only the beginning. We want our children to apply God's word. To do this we will use a simple process called HEAR journaling.

This method of Bible engagement was developed by pastor Robby Gallaty to help disciples move beyond rote reading habits into true engagement with the word.

My children have been encouraged at church and at home to memorize the Scriptures. They have been read the word, taught the word, and had the word exposited for them on many occasions. We also place Scripture passages throughout our home in various artistically pleasing designs (shout out to my wife who rocks at all that stuff). But until my children apply the word of God, it is all irrelevant.

Don't miss this. I have met many people whose children have decided to walk away from the faith, despite these parents doing everything they could to raise them to follow Jesus. I have had conversations with these broken moms and dads as they struggled with the choices their kids are making. I have prayed with them, pleading for the Lord to draw their children to himself. If I could take those parents back to when their children were young and tell them only one thing, it would be this: teach your children to apply the word of God, not just read it.

Think about the Pharisees for a moment, the most religious people on the planet at the time of Jesus. When Jesus talks to the Pharisees, he says these haunting words to them in John 5:39:

> *You pore over the Scriptures because you think you have eternal life in them, and yet they testify about me.*

If the most religious people could pore over the Scriptures and miss God himself, then there has to be more than mere reading in order for a disciple to flourish. We must apply the word, not simply read it. The *HEAR* method is a strategy that is simple and helpful to engage with the word. *HEAR* stands for *Highlight, Explain, Apply,* and *Respond.* Let's take a look at how the method works, then we will learn how to teach it to our children. As you read the word, take notes or journal in the following way:

HIGHLIGHT. After praying for the Holy Spirit's guidance, open your device, notebook, or journal and write the letter H at the top left-hand corner. This exercise will remind you to read with a purpose. In the course of your reading, one or two verses will usually stand out and speak to you. After reading the passage of Scripture, highlight each verse that speaks to you by copying it under the letter H. Record the following:

- The passage of Scripture

- The chapter and verse numbers that especially speak to you

- A title to describe the passage

EXPLAIN. After you have "highlighted" the passage, write the letter E under the previous entry. Now you will explain what the text means. By asking some simple questions, with the help of God's Spirit, you can understand the meaning of a passage or verse. Here are a few questions you can ask of any text:

- To whom was it originally written?

- How does it fit with the verses before and after it?

- Why did the Holy Spirit include this passage in the book?

- What does the Spirit intend to communicate through this text?

APPLY. After writing a brief summary of what you think the text means, write the letter A. This application is the heart of the process. Everything you have done so far culminates under this heading. As you have done before, answer a series of questions to uncover the significance of these verses to you personally:

- How can this help me?

- What does this mean today?

- What would the application of this verse look like in my life?

- What does this mean to me?

- What is God saying to me?

These questions bridge the gap between the ancient world and your world today. They provide a way for God to speak to you from the specific passage or verse. Challenge yourself to write between two and five sentences about how the text applies to your life.

RESPOND. Below the first three entries, write the letter R for respond. Your response to the passage may take on many forms. You may write a call to action. You may describe how you will be different because of what God has said to you through his word. You may indicate what you are going to do because of what you have learned. You may respond by writing a prayer to God. For example, you may ask God to help you to be more loving or to increase your desire to tell others about Jesus.

God does not want us to sit back and wait for him to drop truth into our laps.

Keep in mind that this is your response to what you have just read. Notice that all of the words in the *HEAR* formula are action words: *Highlight, Explain, Apply,* and *Respond.* God does not want us to sit back and wait for him to drop truth into our laps. Instead of waiting passively, God wants us to pursue him actively. Scripture is very clear about this:

> *You will seek me and find me when you search for me with all your heart. (Jeremiah 29:13)*

> *But you, man of God, flee from these things, and pursue righteousness, godliness, faith, love, endurance, and gentleness. (1 Timothy 6:11)*

> *But seek first the kingdom of God and his righteousness,*
> *and all these things will be provided for you.*
>
> *(Matthew 6:33)*

Actively seeking God and pursuing his ways is how we live out what we've read. This is how we go beyond reading alone.

In order to engage with God's word effectively, you need a plan and a strategy. The strategy accomplishes the plan. The *HEAR* method is our strategy, but you and your children need a Bible-reading plan to follow. I suggest that you are on the same plan as your children to maximize the accountability and opportunities to connect. You can use any plan you like, including starting in Genesis 1 and doing a chapter or two every day. The best plans I've used are the Foundations 260 and Foundations 260 New Testament from Replica Ministries. These plans are easy to follow and work great for busy families by providing a digestible amount of reading each day while leaving the weekends open to catch up.

Start helping your child engage with God's word by teaching them to *"Highlight"* a passage. If your children are younger, you can help them choose a passage. If they are older you may want to let them read and choose their own. The primary goal is to help them identify a short passage or verse that sticks out in their reading. If they aren't ready to choose one, pick one for them, at first, to help them with this process.

Once you or your child has chosen a passage, have them list the reference, date, and title for their HEAR journal. Next help them work through the *"Explain"* portion of the method. Ask them questions or tell the insights that you know if they are not yet ready to respond. Remember, this is the part of the process where you list the author, audience, passages before and after the selection, and meaning of the passage. This is one of the more difficult aspects of the *HEAR* method, so make sure you help your child often and provide enough guidance for them at their stage of maturity.

Now that your child has a general understanding of the passage, help him or her determine some applications of the passage. Guide them with these questions:

- Is there an action I need to take?

- Is there a promise I need to claim?

- What is God telling all believers to do as a result of the passage?

- What does this verse look like in my life?

The answers to these questions help your child understand how God's word applies.

Finish the HEAR journal by helping your child *Respond* to the word in a specific way. For younger children, a prayer is often the best response. Help them reword one of the application points in a prayer to the Lord. Or have them write out a prayer about the passage. For older children, help them be more specific in their response. Help them determine an action step they need to take or a promise they can claim from the passage. The key here for parents is to guide your child well based on how mature they are spiritually. If they are a new believer, their responses will often differ from those of a maturing disciple. And that is ok. The *HEAR* method is a process that is learned over time, as is engaging with the word of God. As we grow and apply more of God's word, the word deepens and expands. We never outgrow the Scriptures.

A Daily Practice

When it comes to engaging with the word of God, you need a plan and a strategy. The plan, again, is up to you and you may choose any number of reading plans available. The HEAR journal method is tried and tested. Do not let its simplicity fool you. It is a powerful way to engage with the word.

> **There is no better, more powerful way to lead your children to engage with the word than for them to see you reading your Bible.**

One additional aspect that we must help our children with is consistency. There is no better, more powerful way to lead your children to engage with the word than for them to see you reading your Bible. One way to do this is to pick a place in your home where they will be able to see you each day reading the word. If you start your day with the word, do it at the kitchen table or a common area in your home. When your children wake up, they will see you in the word. They may not mention it, but your example speaks volumes to them about what is important. Some children want to emulate their parents in this practice immediately whereas some might never engage when you do. But they will never forget the model of their parent prioritizing God's word in their life as a daily practice.

Sample HEAR Journal 1
READ: 1 John 5

DATE: April 11, 2022

H (HIGHLIGHT)

"This is the confidence we have before him: If we ask anything according to his will, he hears us. And if we know that he hears whatever we ask, we know that we have what we have asked of him." (1 John 5:14–15)

E (EXPLAIN)

Verses like these can be confusing because the idea of a God who gives us whatever we want is attractive. The key in this passage is "according to his will." The idea may be summarized like this: make your wants God's wants, and then ask for whatever you want.

A (APPLY)

I find myself wanting all sorts of things. Sometimes it's something different every day. I need to focus on aligning myself with God's will so that when I ask something, it's already something that he wants too. His ways are higher than mine, so are his wants higher than my wants.

R (RESPOND)

Father, make me more like you in every way—in my thoughts, actions, and desires. Make the desires of my heart the same things your heart desires, so that I can devote myself to the things that bring you joy.

Sample HEAR Journal 2
READ: Philippians 4:10-13

DATE: August 31, 2022

H (HIGHLIGHT)
"I am able to do all things through him who strengthens me" (Philippians 4:13).

E (EXPLAIN)
Paul was telling the church at Philippi that he had discovered the secret of contentment. No matter the situation in Paul's life, he realized that Christ was all he needed, and Christ was the one who strengthened him to persevere through difficult times.

A (APPLY)
In my life I will experience many ups and downs. My contentment isn't found in circumstances. Rather, it's based on my relationship with Jesus Christ. Only Jesus gives me the strength I need to be content in every circumstance of life.

R (RESPOND)
Lord Jesus, please help me as I strive to be content in you. Through your strength I can make it through any situation I must face.

A few years ago, I challenged my kids, Caedmon and Honor, to meet with me once a week to talk about how we could live out what God was teaching us. We chose a reading plan and determined to do a few HEAR journals a week. When we met, we would pray, talk about our highs and lows of the week, then discuss our HEAR journals. It was a challenge keeping them from criticizing each other's journal. More challenging was to help them understand that we were encouraging one another to apply the word, not playing the role of Holy Spirit in each other's lives. Despite these challenges, it was so powerful to how God moved in their hearts to put his word into practice.

My daughter, being only nine at the time, would bring very short HEAR journals to these meetings. Her content was guided by insights from me, since I didn't expect her to fully understand the context of some of the passages we read. My son, twelve at the time, was able to bring more extensive journals to the meetings. Regardless, the goal with HEAR journals isn't to master journaling, it's to provide a space to record what God is saying to you so you can act upon it. Even more importantly, it provided an opportunity for us to hold one another accountable to the word of God in our lives.

How you teach your children to engage with the word will have a life-long impact on them.

My encouragement to you is to use HEAR journaling as a tool to help your children engage with God's word. Start small. You can have high expectations, but remember you are trying to help them move further toward Bible engagement, not checking off boxes on a homework task. How you teach them to engage with the word will have a life-long impact on them. Work at their pace. Move at the speed of their growth. And watch as God's word does the work, changing them and molding them to be like Jesus.

Write It on Their Hearts

- Purchase your child a Bible that they will use. This may mean getting one designed for children. Consider Bible apps for children who might prefer to engage through technology versus the printed page.

- Choose a place where your children can see you reading your Bible consistently.

- Spend a week or two focused on just one facet of the *HEAR* method (*Highlight, Explain, Apply,* and *Respond*). Really help your child understand how each one works so they can engage with the Scriptures better.

- Purchase a journal for your child to use for their HEAR journaling. Help them use it until they are able to do it on their own.

- Encourage Bible engagement without making it a rote habit with the goal of checking a box. Help them engage with the word at their own pace. You don't want to discourage them by nagging them when they aren't reading or journaling as much as you think they should. It will take time for them to realize their full potential in this discipline.

- If your children are younger, read the Bible to them either daily or regularly.

- Find and use a reading plan that keeps your whole family on the same page. This way you can have conversations about your reading and help each other stay on track.

- Be more focused on the application of the Scriptures than the amount of reading. The goal is to live it out, not just gain head knowledge.

- If your children are older, plan to meet every once in a while, to discuss HEAR journals together and share what you are learning and applying.

6. Over and Over Again

Hold Them Accountable

I thought I was going to die.

It all started two days prior at a theme park in Tampa, Florida. My daughter Honor was celebrating turning ten years old. She and I were on her father/daughter trip to "wherever she wanted to go in the world" (within financial reason). She had chosen a three-theme park circuit across central Florida. At that first park, we walked in the main entrance to see one of the highest, scariest-looking roller coasters she had ever seen. "I am not riding that one!" Honor exclaimed.

"Just give it some time, you don't have to ride anything you don't want to," I told her. I knew it would take a few smaller rides to prepare her to take the leap to something that big. We rode a few rides, walked through the park and enjoyed the day. But she kept looking at that one big scary coaster every time we got near it. We worked our way up to a ride that was a bit more aggressive and as we were getting ready to blast off into a 60-mile per hour launch, she took my hand. I sensed she was scared. I said, "Honor, if they weren't safe, they wouldn't let us ride it. This giant harness that holds us in place will keep us secure no matter how crazy it gets." She nodded and screamed with delight as we rode through the loops and turns at an incredible speed.

It was getting late in the day, and I told her that we would have to leave soon. If we wanted to ride that one big scary ride, we would have to decide now. Honor said she wanted to go and take a look at it up close. We approached the coaster and watched as it roared over us, its passengers screaming through giant loops and inversions. "Ok, let's try it once," she said hesitantly. We boarded the coaster, pulled down our harness and buckled in for the ride. I could tell she was extra nervous. I patted her leg as we began an ascent to the top of the ride. Without notice, the coaster shot straight down and into seven gravity-defying inversions and three enormous loops. Honor yelled at the top of her lungs with excitement. The coaster came to a stop, and she looked at me and said, "Let's do that again!" We did it again. Four more times. She was hooked on this big extreme ride by the time we had to leave.

Our first park was behind us, and she was loving every minute of it. Two days later we were on a new ride in a new park and this one was scaring me. I was in fear for my life. I thought I was going to die. This coaster was the "longest, fastest, and highest ride in the state of Florida," according to the sign. I clung to the harness with a death grip, heart kicking. When we finished, Honor asked to go again. I said, "I don't think I want to go on that again. That was too much for me."

Honor looked at me and, as she does so often, repeated my own words back to me, "Dad, if it wasn't safe, they wouldn't let us ride it." She had a point. I reflected on that as I watched her ride, without me, a few more times. This was a perfect lesson in accountability. Let me explain.

Accountability is a negative word in our culture. It comes across as a statement about keeping people in line. Ensuring we don't do wrong. But in the words of Brian Moran, author of *The 12 Week Year*, accountability isn't about holding people accountable.[7] It's about holding people capable. Think about that. When you are being accountable, you aren't trying to avoid wrong, you are getting help to do what you should do, what you can do, what you are capable of doing. When we think of accountability as a parent, we are trying to hold our children capable of what God created them for. It changes the way we see accountability.

When we think of accountability as a parent, we are trying to hold our children capable of what God created them for.

Like that harness on the roller coaster, we are positioning our children to experience life at its fullest. The harness is a restraint, that is clear. The restraint isn't in place to restrict the high-speed ride, but to empower it. Accountability is the harness that empowers our children to fully experience the life God has for them. From the safety of God's boundaries, we unleash the true freedom God wants us to enjoy. Life will have its high-speed inversions and giant scary loops. Obeying God's commands doesn't lessen our experience, it allows us to live fully in him. Accountability empowers us on the journey to be fully alive in Christ. Hebrews 10:23-24 clarifies how we spur one another on in accountability:

> *Let us hold on to the confession of our hope without wavering, since he who promised is faithful. And let us consider one another in order to provoke love and good works.*

We are to hold one another accountable. The purpose is not to stifle life, but to provoke love and good works. Our culture would tell us accountability is restrictive and something to avoid. After all, it doesn't sound fun and inclusive. The culture would teach our children that being held capable by their parents is squashing their freedom and killing their individuality. However, we must see accountability as a tool to help our children hold on to their confession of hope, not to create legalistic boundaries for the sake of control. It is a means by which we help them sharpen their faith. A tool with which we urge them on toward spiritual growth and restoration with the Lord.

Accountability empowers us on the journey to be fully alive in Christ.

Holding Your Children Capable
In this age of hectic schedules and technology there are a multitude of things that distract us. Social media, games, devices, screens, and a culture that celebrates narcissism

create the perfect storm of options that fill our lives with distraction. As parents, we must help our children live out their faith within this storm. Accountability provides a means by which we help them stay on track to run the race well. In our home we have strategies in place.

- We schedule "alone time" for them to disconnect.

- We incorporate tools like Bark, Covenant Eyes, and Screen Time to help them traverse the often-chaotic world of technology.

- We intentionally work with them on spiritual habits like Bible reading and Scripture memory.

- We prioritize church engagement and spiritual growth.

- We encourage hard work and a servant attitude.

- We assign daily and weekly chores and tasks at home.

- We make discussion about life challenges a regular occurrence.

Even with these elements in place we struggle, like all families, with boundaries and margins. Our children see what their friends get to do and ask why they can't. They struggle with obedience like we all do. They question rules and directions. They have many opinions. While we don't have all the answers and sometimes our leadership as parents isn't what it needs to be, we press on. This is the hard work of accountability: consistency. "I've told them a hundred times to do that," or "We have been over this again and again, do I need to explain it more?"

The answer is yes. Accountability requires us as parents to press in over and over again. Think about your own heart and your own obedience to the Father. If you are like me, you struggle just as much, if not more, with his direction as your children do with yours. But we don't give up, we press on in our own spiritual journey of sanctification.

Accountability requires us as parents to press in over and over again.

The tool we will use to help with accountability is based on spurring your children on to follow Jesus and be like him. This is a journey that takes a lifetime: your whole life, and their whole lives. The goal is to lead them while they are young, so they do not stray when they are older. It isn't easy, and at times may seem far beyond what we are capable of doing. But let me attempt to hold you capable as a parent. The Lord blessed you with your children and he will empower you, through his Holy Spirit, to hold them capable. Not of your own flesh and ability, nor their flesh or ability, but through the power of Christ in you. That same Jesus lives in them if they are a believer.

SPUR

There are five steps to help you *SPUR* your children on. They are: *Sharpen, Pray, Urge,* and *Restore.*

SHARPEN. To sharpen iron, one must use more iron. Imagine a knife blade rubbing against another knife blade. The blades sharpen one another. As a believer you are to sharpen other believers. While at times one is forming and sharpening the other, both blades benefit, and both are necessary. If a knife isn't sharpened, it is still a knife, but it is far less effective as a dull blade. This is mutual accountability. For you to speak truth into the life of your child and hold them capable of all God has for them, you will have to do the hard work of sharpening. The beauty is that through the process, you too will be sharpened. Proverbs 27:17 states this simple truth clearly:

Iron sharpens iron, and one person sharpens another.

The benefit of a sharp knife is that it can do its work more effectively. We want to help our children, as tools of the Lord, to do his will more effectively. And while we press in to sharpen them, we are sharpened in the process.

But what does sharpening look like in day-to-day life? It starts with listening. That's right, before we take action, we need to be able to hear our child's heart and understand their motives. All too often we jump to correct wrongs and provide direction. Those things are needed, but in order to be effective, we need to understand the perspective.

My son, Caedmon, often antagonizes his little sister. Whether it's a snide comment or an intentional barb, he takes delight in frustrating her. Now he doesn't do this all the time, and, on the whole, he is a good big brother. But he has his moments. When he does this, I typically go straight to, "Why did you do that, son?" My tone is usually one of consternation and frustration. It is also followed by, "Go to your room," or "No more screen time for you today." My wife's response, which is far more Christ-like than mine, is to have a conversation with him, without a hostile tone. She asks much better questions:

- Would you like it if someone treated you that way?

- Can you see how you hurt your sister by doing this?

- How can we work together to avoid this behavior again?

We must learn to navigate correction with a focus on helping and spiritual growth.

Now I am not saying he doesn't still get consequences for his actions, but you can see how these two responses might yield different results. My harsh response might be right, but it doesn't sharpen him and teach him. My wife's more intentional approach provides the iron needed to sharpen him and help him grow. It doesn't happen in one instance, but over time, both parent and child grow in relationship, connection, and response.

To apply the Proverbs 27:17 principle of iron sharpening iron we must be more intentional than ever. We must learn to navigate correction with a focus on helping and spiritual growth. The balance is no easy task. But you are capable of it and with prayer and intentionality, you can

grow to do it well, just as your children will grow and learn more effectively.

PRAY. The role of prayer in accountability cannot be overstated. Depending on where you're at in your journey, you may have had some of the greatest struggles you've ever faced as a parent. If your children are younger, you may have yet to face significant challenges. Regardless, there will be issues and there will be battles. The way to *SPUR* your children on in accountability is through prayer.

James 5:16 says,

> *Therefore, confess your sins to one another and pray for one another, so that you may be healed. The prayer of a righteous person is very powerful in its effect.*

Notice the connection between prayer and confession of sins. We hold our children capable by praying for them when they fall. By sharing struggles with one another, families are able to pray with specificity. Knowing struggles allows us to be more intentional in praying for the need. Accountability is ownership. Helping our children own their faith means praying them through the areas where they face the most battles.

When my children and I gather for our discipleship group time, as mentioned earlier, we make note of at least one area we need help in. For my youngest, the issues were related to how she should respond to God. "I'm not reading my Bible consistently," and "I need to share my faith." With my older child, the issues were more connected to the Bible passages we studied together. "I need to have a better attitude," and "I should be nicer to my sister."

These simple requests allowed them to verbalize their struggles so we could make note and pray for one another. I would share my needs as well. I asked for prayer about being angry and my attitude while driving. They were able to pray for me and spur me on in accountability too. One of the great side effects is that as a family we all become more aware of each other's weaknesses and needs. Not only can we then make it a matter of prayer but we also encourage and spur one another on to run the race before us.

URGE. The process of holding our children accountable will not always be easy. "Sharpening" can be painful as we lean in to help our children. As we, along with our kids, seek to run the race well, prayer is crucial in seeking the Lord's guidance. Next, we move on to *Urge*. Ephesians 4:1-3 says,

> *Therefore I, the prisoner in the Lord, urge you to walk worthy of the calling you have received, with all humility and gentleness, with patience, bearing with one another in love, making every effort to keep the unity of the Spirit through the bond of peace.*

There is plenty to unpack from this verse, but I want to focus on one key phrase: "walk worthy." My guess is you have urged your children many times:

- Urged them to brush their teeth.
- Urged them to do their homework.
- Urged them to stop pestering their sibling.
- Urged them to clean up their room.
- Urged them to give it their best in sports or competitions.

But when was the last time you urged them to walk worthy? If it's been a while, or maybe even never, then you are not alone. Regardless, this is a crucial part of accountability in the life of a believer.

When was the last time you urged your child to walk worthy?

The word urge simply means to "urgently and persistently persuade someone to do something."[8] At least, that's the verb for urge. The noun, on the other hand, is to "have a strong desire or impulse."[9] Isn't it interesting that as a verb it is used to persuade someone toward an action, while as a noun, it is the desire of someone to take action. As parents we urge (verb) our children to walk worthy, so that they will have the urge (noun) to walk worthy.

Walk worthy of what? The calling you have received. In order to hold our children capable and enact effective accountability, parents must urge them on. This is not the same as sharpening. This is persuasion. Persuasion means we are helping them understand why it is important. When I am urging my children to walk worthy, it often looks something like the following scenario. When they are watching or want to watch something objectionable, I ask:

- Does this TV show glorify the things of the world over the things of God?

- What good things can we learn from this and apply in our lives?

- If we can't, should we even engage with it?

Notice that this interaction wasn't me telling them the show was bad or wrong. Even if it is, and even if I might eventually get there in this conversation, what I want to do initially is help them see that for themselves. I want to persuade them to look at it through a biblical lens. The series of questions I chose were designed to get them thinking and get them to take steps toward walking worthy. Let's look at another example. One child makes fun of, or picks on, the other. Here is what we can ask:

- How would Jesus treat his sibling?

- What kinds of words would he use in a conversation with them?

- Why is it important to build one another up rather than tear each other down?

Again, I am not saying there wouldn't be additional consequences for wrong actions, but primarily I am concerned with urging my child to walk worthy. The goal is to help them see the situation from a Christ-centered angle and persuade them that his ways are better than ours.

If we only ever respond with anger, frustration, and consequences, we will miss the many opportunities to persuade and urge them to instead walk worthy. This may be a long and painful process for some children, but the goal, as always, is to present their hearts with the opportunity for God to write his word on it. It won't be a one-time event, but purposeful engagement over time.

RESTORE. The final step is to *Restore*. Galatians 6:1-2 teaches us,

> *Brothers and sisters, if someone is overtaken in any wrongdoing, you who are spiritual, restore such a person with a gentle spirit, watching out for yourselves so that you also won't be tempted. Carry one another's burdens; in this way you will fulfill the law of Christ.*

What a powerful and hopeful passage of Scripture. We are to restore those who fall, with a gentle spirit. We are to carry one another's burdens. When I reflect on this passage it reminds me of the cross. Jesus, without sin, carried the burdens of the world on his shoulders to restore sinners. Accountability should always lead to restoration. Again, we are holding our children capable. What has God designed them to be? How has God shaped them and what does God want to do with them? This isn't a capability that is derived from our own flesh to accomplish anything. This is living in Christ, empowered by the Holy Spirit, to experience the fullness of life he promises.

As parents we must endeavor to restore our children when they fall. Recently, one of my children chose to disobey and pursue something we had warned about. When we confronted our child about their choice, they broke down and began to cry. My wife held our child and prayed about the choice. We followed it up with a conversation from a loving, connected perspective. The regret was evident, but we wanted to move our child past regret to repentance. Restoration happens when there is repentance, not just regret. Everyone regrets getting caught; a child of God moves to repentance as the Holy Spirit convicts.

Accountability is one of the most critical aspects of discipling your children. We must *SPUR* our children on to run their race and pursue Jesus. We will regularly need to press in when our children stray, when they need encouragement, or when they simply need to learn truth to apply to their lives. Parenting is a full-time job and, as we have learned, discipling your children only adds to the complexity. But just as athletes at the highest level are honed through intentional accountability in their training, our children need parents who are ready to take on the task of spurring them on in Christ. The Holy Spirit will empower you; the word is sufficient to equip you. Now, it is up to you to take on the task and hold your children capable of experiencing full life in Christ.

Write It on Their Hearts

- Discuss and plan spiritual activities with your children. Scripture memory, Bible reading, and church involvement are all spiritually healthy habits. By discussing these activities, you and your child can work together to help one another stay accountable.

- Set a reminder on your phone to encourage your child daily and/or weekly in their pursuit of Christ. Ask questions like, "How can I help you focus on the Lord this week?" or "What has God been teaching you lately?"

- Help your children develop goals in their spiritual life and *SPUR* them on to walk worthy. Some examples are:

- read through the New Testament in a year

- memorize passages of Scripture

- identify a lost friend and share the gospel with them

- have a consistent time with the Lord daily.

- Help your children make the connection between their giftedness and how the Lord can use that for his glory. Find moments to encourage and remind them of that connection.

- Share and discuss HEAR journals with your children on a regular basis (chapter 5).

- Consider using technology that helps with accountability. Apps like Covenant Eyes, Bark, and Accountable2You are some examples. Discuss these with your child so they know you are there to help them be accountable with devices.

- Discuss with your spouse how you will handle situations when your child struggles or strays. Having a plan before things happen will help you handle them more effectively.

- Share your goals and struggles with your child so they can encourage and help you be accountable in your life. This will help encourage them to be a part of the process rather than only a recipient of accountability. Work together as iron sharpens iron.

7. The Hardest Work You'll Ever Do

Teach Them to Rest

Restlessness is an addiction. Hurry is the drug. We feed our need to stay busy by packing our schedules beyond our capacity. We have no margin. No time to spare. We believe all this will stop our restlessness or make us happy or pacify our desire to achieve. But it doesn't; it just makes us busier. It gives us a topic for conversation and it provides the watching world with the appearance that we are effective, successful, and winning at life. And it's not just the world watching, our kids are also watching. They are learning our ways. Parents, are we contributing to our kids' restlessness with our busy schedules.

It was a crazy Thursday night. Every Thursday was crazy during this season. Our daughter, Honor, was in gymnastics from 6-7 p.m. Our son, Caedmon, had Jiu Jitsu class from 6:30-7:30 p.m. My wife Melissa and I, meanwhile, were doing premarital counseling for a couple from 6-7:30 p.m. It took a colossal amount of effort to make this schedule feasible. The house had to be straightened up for guests. Dinner had to be prepared and completed earlier than our typical evening. Rides with friends had to be coordinated. Work issues cropped up from time to time taking either Melissa or me out of the team effort.

We had readied the kids for their rides that evening. Prepped and scarfed down dinner. Did a hurried, just barely acceptable pass on the house cleaning. The kids were flustered because we had to rush them through dinner and prep them for their separate events. I got mad because things weren't going well, and we were all rushed. Melissa was frustrated with me because I was getting mad and taking it out on everyone else.

Finally, the kids' ride showed up and we sent them off. I initiated a last-minute glance at the book we were working through for the pre-marital counseling session and sat down just as the doorbell rang. Our friends arrived and took a seat. We spent a few minutes chatting and turned our discussion to the assigned reading.

The topic was on prioritizing family and protecting boundaries to create margin. As we discussed how to work on this, using examples from our marriage, I couldn't help but feel hypocritical. Here I was trying to help someone else navigate busyness and hurry; in the midst of busyness and hurry. The irony was palpable.

While this type of evening might have been an exception instead of the rule for our family, more often than not, it is a standard evening for many families. Parents and kids go to separate sports or events, rarely sitting down to dinner or spending the evening together. Our culture tells us this schedule is normal. Applauded, even. I dare say that might have also been the case in ancient Jerusalem when Mr. The Great set up his new society with more to be consumed. Take heart that we are not the first parents to struggle with hurry, and we won't be the last.

Hurry addiction is such a problem that God commanded us to rest.

Hurry addiction is such a problem that God commanded us to rest. In Exodus 20:8-11 the fourth commandment says,

> *Remember the Sabbath day, to keep it holy: You are to labor six days and do all your work, but the seventh day is a Sabbath to the LORD your God. You must not do any work—you, your son or daughter, your male or female servant, your livestock, or the resident alien who is within your city gates. For the LORD made the heavens and the earth, the sea, and everything in them in six days; then he rested on the seventh day. Therefore the LORD blessed the Sabbath day and declared it holy.*

God commands us to rest and emulates it for us. He concluded creation of the universe with rest. God, he who needs no rest, rested. Jesus reemphasized this in his ministry. So how do we teach our children to observe the command to rest? How do we help them break the cycle of hurry addiction and busyness that plagues our culture? What follows is an acronym I've developed that makes some biblical principles easy to remember. Together, they form the word *STOP*.

Still

Psalm 46:10 presents a powerful strategy for stopping and resting.

Be still, and know that I am God.
I will be exalted among the nations,
I will be exalted in the earth! (ESV)

In that introductory sentence we find the powerful words, "Be still." Stillness is very, very difficult for a hurried culture. If you have young children, you might even look at those words and roll your eyes or laugh with fond memories of what stillness used to mean. I get it, there are seasons when we are busier than others. There are days when stillness is so far from our reality that we wonder if it ever existed at all. The great irony is that finding and practicing stillness takes more hard work and effort than being busy.

Coupled in the first line of the psalm we discover that stillness and recognition of God go hand in hand. The secret then, is to attain stillness by recognizing that only God is God. What does that mean? Only God can be God. Only he can know everything, be everywhere, and accomplish any task. The big theological words are omniscient, omnipresent, and omnipotent. In recognizing this about God, we can find stillness.

We must teach our children that they don't have to have all the answers, be at all the stuff, or do all the things. None of that is required in order to glorify the Lord. He *will* be exalted! The weight is lifted from our shoulders when we realize that this is God's role, not ours. This recognition leads us to being still and finding rest in that truth. Often, our restlessness is a result of trying to do what God does. When we recognize that God is in control, we can pause and reflect on his sufficiency. This is how we exalt him.

Often, our restlessness is a result of trying to do what God does.

Cultivating stillness in your children takes place when you model this for them. A powerful practice I have learned and passed on to my children is called centering prayer. It is a very simple process where you really slow down, be quiet, and get still with the Lord. First, you'll need a quiet place. I recommend teaching them this in their bedroom so they can keep practicing it when they are there alone. Have them close their eyes and state the first line of Psalm 46:10: "Be still, and know that I am God." Then repeat the process after a breath or two of silence but remove one word or phrase at a time. The end result looks like this:

Say: *Be still, and know that I am God.*

Pause for a silent moment.

Say: *Be still, and know that I am.*

Pause for a silent moment.

Say: *Be still, and know.*

Pause for a silent moment.

Say: *Be still.*

Pause for a silent moment.

Say: *Be.*

Pause for a silent moment. Make this final moment last a while.

On your first attempt, try for one minute of uninterrupted silence. As you continue this practice, extend that final moment to five or even ten minutes as your child's ability to be still grows. This simple tool helps them focus on the word. It allows the word of God to guide their heart as they rest in him. Once they have practiced this and are comfortable with it, move on to the next phase of the *STOP* process: *Talk*.

Talk

Right out of the gate, this seems weird. How does talking help my child find rest? Philippians 4:6-7 teaches us,

> *Don't worry about anything, but in everything, through prayer and petition with thanksgiving, present your requests to God. And the peace of God, which surpasses all understanding, will guard your hearts and minds in Christ Jesus.*

Prayer is pivotal in our relationship with the Lord. As it applies to rest, notice that the passage says, "The peace of God ... will guard your hearts and minds in Christ Jesus." Through prayer, Jesus gives us peace. A peace for our mind and heart. With our minds we overthink, we fixate on issues, and we get distracted by "what ifs" and "why nots." With our hearts we are passionate and emotional.

The Scriptures say the heart is deceitful (Jeremiah 17:9). It lies to us by telling us that our desires are greater than what God has for us. Both our mind and heart create chaos. They are two robbers living within us, drawing us away from the Lord. But through prayer—talking with God—we can receive peace. Peace that guards our heart and our mind. This cannot be overstated; prayer is the key to rest. Prayer moves the focus from us to the Lord. Prayer gives us the opportunity to say what we need to say to the only one who can give us real peace regardless of the circumstance.

As part of the *STOP* process, move from the stillness of the centering prayer to spending a few minutes talking to God about all the things going on in your life. Everything on your mind and every emotion in your heart, lay it all before the Lord. Then, accept his peace knowing that the Creator of the universe has heard you and he is in control of it all.

This cannot be overstated; prayer is the key to rest.

As you walk with your children through this step, give them some examples of what to say to God as they talk. Use your own situations to help them see how practical and real these conversations can be.

- Lord, I can't stop thinking about the upcoming business meeting I have. Will you give me comfort and peace about it?

- Father, when I'm driving, my heart desires to be angry with others on the road. I don't want to have that anger anymore. Will you free me from that wrong attitude?

- Jesus, help me have peace so I can rest in you no matter how difficult today may seem.

These are some practical examples but take it even further by asking them what issues they may have on their heart or mind and then help them craft a sentence to pray to the Lord relative to their needs. Once you've spent a few minutes talking to the Lord, move on to the next part: *Offer*.

Offer

First, we get still, then we talk to the Lord in prayer, next we offer our cares, our anxieties, by casting them on the Lord. 1 Peter 5:6-7 says,

> *Humble yourselves, therefore, under the mighty hand of God, so that he may exalt you at the proper time, casting all your cares on him, because he cares about you.*

Research shows that children born since 2000 are facing a significant rise in anxiety and depression.[10] These findings point toward the role of technology in regard to social interaction as a primary cause. Social status is more prevalent in an always "on" culture.

Prior to this current social media age, teens and preteens were generally limited to one community in their social interactions. So, children were operating within a smaller group of peers as their social lives developed. Now everyone's life is available for all to see. The social exposure of anyone with a device can become national and potentially even global.

Regardless of your perspective on social media and how online culture has made an impact on children, the reality is that anxiety among these groups is at an all-time high. While we may not be able to change any of those components, we can, as believers, obey the word in how we help them handle it. We cast our cares, our anxieties on the Lord. We offer our struggles over to he who cares for us. This can be done by expanding our prayer to share these burdens. We begin with stillness, we move into talking with the Lord, and we name those anxieties that we need him to address. Some examples are below:

"Lord, I am struggling with the way my friends treat me."

"Jesus, take the burden of my desire to be known by others and remind me that I am known by you."

"Father, help me deal with the pressure of this week's schedule."

Again, help your children voice these concerns at first by modeling this offering in your own prayer. Explain how we can give all of our challenges and issues to the Lord. Then help them craft these sentences with their own concerns. Start with a simple sentence and help them grow in their communication with the Lord during this slowed-down stillness. Once they have learned this practice, help them move on to the final phase: *Peace*.

Peace

One of the most powerful aspects of finding rest in the Lord, is the peace that he offers us. John 14:27 tells us,

Peace I leave with you. My peace I give to you. I do not give to you as the world gives. Don't let your heart be troubled or fearful.

Finding rest in Jesus results in peace. He gives us a peace that is beyond what the world has to offer. We can comfort our children, but only God can give them a peace that takes away trouble and fear. Help your kids grow in acceptance of his peace by verbalizing this truth. Sometimes we say it, believing it even when we don't feel it. Teach your children that feelings are fleeting and often deceitful. The truth is in God's word. It comes from Jesus as he empowers us through his Holy Spirit. As followers of Jesus, we stand on what he is saying in spite of how the world and our circumstances make us feel. A couple of suggestions are:

> "Lord, thank you for giving me peace even when it feels like things are hectic."

> "Jesus, let me rest in your peace and reflect on your word and truth."

> "Holy Spirit, give me strength to know that you are with me, and peace is found in you and not my circumstances."

These simple statements help us say what our heart might not be feeling. The process may take time as God works to give us his peace. We are equipping our children to implement this kind of response to their struggles. We then trust the Lord to do what only he can do in their lives.

As followers of Jesus, we stand on what he is saying in spite of how the world and our circumstances make us feel.

Putting all the elements together, help your children practice the *STOP* process consistently.

It may start with stillness for a few moments weekly and expand to include every step. I suggest picking a time each day to implement the practice. Choose a time that works for you and your children. It could be a bedtime ritual or a way to start your day. The goal is to help them learn the process and then empower them to practice it consistently on their own as time goes on.

- *Still*: be still and engage in centering prayer.

- *Talk*: reach out to the Lord in prayer and reflective silence.

- *Offer*: specifically offer up anxieties and issues you face by name to the Lord.

- *Peace*: verbalize your acceptance of the peace Jesus promises every believer.

The whole process might take only a few minutes at first. But as it becomes a common practice, watch how the Lord uses this time to help your child find rest.

Write It on Their Hearts

- If your child is very young, practice the *STOP* with them. Creating this rhythm in your life will make it easier to help them implement it once they are old enough.

- Help your child identify a place where they can get still. It may be their bedroom or the back porch.

- Spend time with your child in their chosen location, helping them practice the *STOP* process one small step at a time. It may take a few days or even weeks to become solidified in their life.

- Have a discussion with your child about some of the things that make them anxious. Help them identify and verbalize these so they can pray about them with you and eventually on their own.

- Determine how technology might play a role in anxiety and distraction in their life. Discuss how you can develop tactics to minimize or better control the influence of technology. Keep in mind that technology isn't the enemy. Like anything else it can become and idol or a tool used by the enemy in our lives.

- Refer back to the chapter on prayer and implement what you've learned there to help them as they talk to God about restlessness.

- Have a discussion with your child about how you can help them slow down and combat hurry. Be honest about the things you struggle with in this area to help them understand how it impacts them, too.

- Pick a window of time or a day of the week when your family might minimize busyness and screen time. Explain that practicing the Sabbath, resting from work and focusing on the Lord, is a healthy pattern for every believer.

Your Family Discipleship Plan

God writes his word on the hearts of our children. We prepare and encourage the process by creating opportunities for it to happen through discipleship. By being with our children intentionally, we live out Deuteronomy 6:4-7:

> Listen, Israel: The LORD our God, the LORD is one. Love the LORD your God with all your heart, with all your soul, and with all your strength. These words that I am giving you today are to be in your heart. Repeat them to your children. Talk about them when you sit in your house and when you walk along the road, when you lie down and when you get up.

By intentionally living out the six elements we've discussed in this book—love, prayer, connection, Scripture, accountability, and rest—we present our children's hearts as a manuscript on which the Lord can write. While you have been presented with many practical ways to implement each element, it may be helpful to have a long-term approach.

Implementation Plans

One very effective way of ensuring you hit all six facets of the discipleship process is to work through each of the six, focusing on each for one month. This would repeat twice a year for a total of two months focused on each element. Simply repeat the process each year you disciple your child. Use the following list as a guide but keep in mind this is a loose structure. Don't feel like you have to be driven by your schedule. Use it as a helpful reminder and guide, not a calendared event that you may struggle to keep up with.

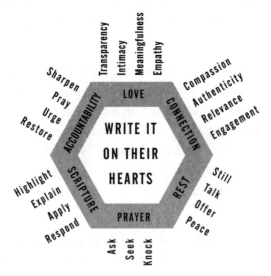

You might choose to focus on each aspect for a week at a time, which would result in the same amount of time spent on each aspect but experienced more frequently. There are built-in breaks, but you can adjust them as needed to fit your schedule.

You could also choose to devote one day a week to each element, giving yourself a weekly rhythm and more predictable schedule. Since there are six elements, that gives you one day a week as a break.

The suggestion for a One Year Plan is outlined on the next page.

Weekly Plan

Monday	Love
Tuesday	Prayer
Wednesday	Connection
Thursday	Scripture
Friday	Accountability
Saturday	Rest
Sunday	*Break*

One Year Plan

Week	Element	Week	Element	Week	Element	Week	Element
1	Love	14	Love	27	Love	40	Love
2	Prayer	15	Prayer	28	Prayer	41	Prayer
3	Connection	16	Connection	29	Connection	42	Connection
4	Scripture	17	Scripture	30	Scripture	43	Scripture
5	Accountability	18	Accountability	31	Accountability	44	Accountability
6	Rest	19	Rest	32	Rest	45	Rest
7	Love	20	Love	33	Love	46	Love
8	Prayer	21	Prayer	34	Prayer	47	Prayer
9	Connection	22	Connection	35	Connection	48	Connection
10	Scripture	23	Scripture	36	Scripture	49	Scripture
11	Accountability	24	Accountability	37	Accountability	50	Accountability
12	Rest	25	Rest	38	Rest	51	Rest
13	BREAK	26	BREAK	39	BREAK	52	BREAK

Tools Option

In these plans, you'll focus on the individual component of each tool mentioned in *Write It on Their Hearts*. Each day you'll think about, pray about, and actively engage with the part of the tool assigned. For example, if *Restore* is the focus of the day, you might determine if there is an area you or your child needs restoration in and make it happen. Or, you may have a conversation with your child about restoration and how you as their parent wants to help them with it. Or you might simply pray that the Lord helps you identify a need for restoration and practice it when the time comes. Don't overthink or overcomplicate each day. Use the plan to remind you of each component and work from there.

Monthly Tools Plan

DAY 1	Love	DAY 16	Authenticity
DAY 2	Prayer	DAY 17	Relevance
DAY 3	Connection	DAY 18	Engagement
DAY 4	Scripture	DAY 19	Highlight
DAY 5	Accountability	DAY 20	Explain
DAY 6	Rest	DAY 21	Apply
DAY 7	*Break*	DAY 22	Respond
DAY 8	Transparency	DAY 23	Sharpen
DAY 9	Intimacy	DAY 24	Pray
DAY 10	Meaningfulness	DAY 25	Urge
DAY 11	Empathy	DAY 26	Restore
DAY 12	Ask	DAY 27	Still
DAY 13	Seek	DAY 28	Talk
DAY 14	Knock	DAY 29	Offer
DAY 15	Connection	DAY 30	Peace

Weekly Discipleship Meeting

Meeting with your child on a weekly basis for about 20-40 minutes can make all the difference as you invest in their life. The focus of this book is that discipleship happens as you spend time with your children. But you may be at a stage where a weekly meeting might increase your impact. That doesn't mean you should exchange a one-time meeting with an ongoing investing lifestyle. But you may want to add this level of intentionality for a season. I'd recommend doing this during ages 8-18 for a six-to-twelve-month window. You should assess your own child's interest and spiritual maturity level for when it could be most effective. Notice the elements involved in the meeting and how each connects:

Lead the meeting with love throughout as it should encompass every area of how we disciple our children.

Order of the Meeting	Time (25-35 minutes)	Discipleship Element
Prayer & silence (centering prayer to start)	3-5 minutes	Prayer/Rest
Share one high and one low of the week	3-5 minutes	Connection
Practice Scripture memory	2 minutes	Scripture/ Accountability
Share HEAR journals	10-15 minutes	Scripture/ Connection
Ask accountability questions	3 minutes	Accountability
Pray together	5 minutes	Prayer

Summary of each component of the Discipleship Time

Prayer & Silence. Spend a short time with centering prayer (chapter 7). If you haven't yet practiced this with your children, you can use this time to teach them. Or you may choose to pray together and use your other intentional time to teach centering prayer and incorporate it later. Don't drag it out. This is a time to settle your mind and heart and prepare for your meeting together, not a time to list every prayer request you have.

Highs and Lows. This is one of my daughter's favorite times. As tempting as it can be to get stuck here, only allow one high point and one low point for each person. And they must be for yourself, not someone else. My daughter once tried to tattle on my wife by using something my wife had done as her low. Nice try, but that's not how this works. Your high and low might be, "My high this week was making s'mores and playing outside with the family. My low this week was a really tough meeting at work." Your child's high and low might look something like, "My high this week was going to my friend's birthday party at the trampoline park. My low was when I forgot to do my chores and got in trouble." This exercise leads to connection because you're practicing *Compassion, Authenticity, Relevance,* and *Engagement* (chapter 4).

Practice Scripture Memory. The first time you meet together, choose a memory verse. The goal will be to each say the verse at your next meeting and then choose a new verse to memorize together. These can be verses you're already working on in your current reading plans. Don't make it cumbersome or more complicated than it needs to be. This exercise is to incorporate *Scripture* (chapter 5) and *Accountability* (chapter 6) by sharing your verses and holding one another capable to do the work of memorizing.

Share HEAR Journals. Each of you should choose one or two HEAR journal entries (chapter 5) to share. Walk through each aspect of the HEAR journal, sharing what you highlighted, explained, how it applies to you, and your response. Each one should take only a few minutes but can be insightful into what is on your child's heart and how they are incorporating Scripture into their lives. It helps develop connection as you share with each other.

Accountability Questions. Move to asking accountability questions. As we strive to *SPUR* our children on (chapter 6), our goal here is to ask questions that hold our children capable as they develop their relationship with Jesus and others. The questions you ask will differ according to the ages of your children. Some examples of accountability questions are:

- How have you encouraged someone this week?

- Have you been tempted to disobey or do something you shouldn't this week? How can I help you avoid that temptation in the future?

- What is a goal I can help you with?

- How can you show kindness to your sibling this week? (Check next week!)

Accountability questions aren't just for the kids. Be prepared to answer each question you ask so your children can help you be accountable. Remember, iron sharpens iron.

Close With Prayer. You or your child close in prayer, or even take turns praying as you finish your meeting. If your children are old enough, you can ask them for specific prayer requests. You can pray for an aspect of the upcoming week, pray for one another's goals for accountability for the week, and pray for any specific prayer requests. If you are asking your children to pray, give them a topic to pray for and take turns praying. Choose the order and ask a child to close or close the prayer yourself. After you ask, remind them to seek during the week and keep knocking on the doors God reveals to us (chapter 3).

From Our Family
to Yours

By Melissa Swain

When Chris and I married in 1998, we had no idea what life and ministry would bring our way. We were young and foolish, but we didn't care. We loved Jesus and each other, and that was enough. We spent a lot of time growing up together over the nearly 23 years we were married. Neither of us saw life playing out like it did. We had plans— few of which actually happened like we imagined. But the Lord was in all of it. And he still is.

Chris Swain was quite possibly the funniest human I've ever met. He was also the most disciplined, intentional person I've ever known. If he decided he was going to do something, he did it, whether it was conquering a video game or launching a new ministry. Regardless of what had come before, he had a way of putting off the old and embracing the new.

All of those things made him a great disciple-maker. Once he determined to invest in someone, he didn't quit. And since he was fun to hang out with, it was never a chore. When we welcomed children into our family, he decided he would be the best dad he could be. And he was. He used all of his experience in life, the United States Marine Corps, and ministry to invest in them. He taught them all that he had learned from the men he admired, and most of all from knowing Jesus.

Watching him grow as a man, minister, husband, and dad has been one of the greatest privileges of my life. I am who I am today because of Chris. He always encouraged me to follow Jesus and pushed me in ways only he could, gently shoving me outside the box I built for myself. He celebrated every victory, large and small, and never made me wonder if I was loved. Our children had the privilege of watching Chris love Jesus, his family, and the church, in that order. Caedmon and Honor never doubted their dad's love and carry his legacy forward daily. I see so much of him in them, but most of all, I see the love he had for Jesus reflected in them.

To say Chris was intentional about discipleship in our home would be an understatement. Even before he worked in a discipleship ministry, Chris operated with a sense of urgency when it came to leading our children to follow Jesus. I had the privilege of walking alongside Chris and learning from his intensely focused mind and heart. We came from vastly different family backgrounds and learned that our differences were not a liability, but possibly our greatest asset. We only had to allow the Lord to show us the path he had for us rather than what we had always known. Chris dreamed of being able to help other parents find their sweet spot with family discipleship without feeling overwhelmed.

This book is Chris's dream made reality and truly an overflow of the conviction and passion he had to help other parents and families pursue Jesus in their homes. Chris was not perfect, and I think the stories he chose to share illustrate that. He certainly could have recounted numerous failures of mine. He reminds us the good news is that we don't have to be perfect to point our kids to Jesus, and in our failures we all learn humility, grace, and forgiveness.

Chris Swain met Jesus face to face on July 15, 2021—much sooner than any of us planned, and still somehow in God's perfect time. But with this book in my hand, I can continue what he started in our home, using his guide to customize the discipleship needs of our family to this new paradigm. Chris's legacy lives not only in us, but in every family who uses this tool in their pursuit of Jesus. May his life and death bring glory to God and may there be generations in heaven because of his passionate obedience.

Melissa Swain

Acknowledgments

Robby Gallaty, thanks for your iron-sharpening-iron friendship with Chris. We never imagined our pastor and boss would be one of his closest friends and best fishing buddy. Ben Trueblood and Greg Westmoreland, thanks for your friendship since the beginning of our ministry days and your input as this book was written and finalized. I am grateful for the men who taught Chris how to care for people and prioritize family: Ronnie Floyd, Shawn Smith, Harold O'Chester, Jeff Young, and many others I haven't the space to list. Jim and Sandy Swain, thank you for always loving and believing in your son. To the staff team at Long Hollow Church, thank you for your support, trust, and willingness to work alongside Chris and each other to further the kingdom.

I am immensely grateful to everyone who prayed for me, cheered me on, and offered assistance as I finished this work Chris began, believing in me when I didn't believe in myself. To our friends who are the family we chose, thank you for your love, prayers, and support, even in the darkest days. Ronnie Floyd, thank you for giving me the experience necessary to complete this project. To my parents, Keith and Cindy Loewer, and my siblings, Kristin, Sarah,

Aaron, Evan, Emily, and Jessica: thank you for always having my back and anything else I need. Chris Swain, thank you for boldly following Jesus and unapologetically leading and intentionally loving our family for nearly 23 years. Your legacy lives on in our two amazing kids. Caedmon and Honor, thank you for sharing your dad with the church and other families your whole lives, and now even in his death, sharing him with the world.

Andrew Wolgemuth, thank you for advocating for this book and for shifting gears to walk alongside me, guiding me through to the finished product. Brian, Carl, James, Bethany, and everyone at The Good Book Company, thank you for believing this book matters to the kingdom.

Endnotes

1 Robby Gallaty, *Here and Now: Thriving in the Kingdom of Heaven Today,* (B&H Books, 2019), p 47.

2 Teaching the Children: Sharp Ideological Differences, Some Common Ground | Pew Research Center https://www.pewresearch.org/politics/2014/09/18/teaching-the-children-sharp-ideological-differences-some-common-ground/ (accessed on Jan. 20, 2022).

3 Christianity Is No Longer Americans' Default Faith - Barna Group https://www.barna.com/research/christianity-is-no-longer-americans-default-faith/ (accessed on Jan. 20, 2022).

4 Robert Gallaty, *Rediscovering Discipleship: Making Jesus' Final Words Our First Work* (Zondervan, 2015), p 130.

5 How Working Parents Share Parenting and Household Responsibilities | Pew Research Center.

6 Intimate | Definition of Intimate by Merriam-Webster.

7 Brian P. Moran, Michael Lennington, *The 12 Week Year: Get More Done in 12 Weeks than Others Do in 12 Months,* (Wiley Publishing, 2013).

8 https://www.lexico.com/en/definition/urge (accessed Mar. 2, 2022).

9 https://www.lexico.com/en/definition/urge (accessed Mar. 2, 2022).

10 https://worldhappiness.report/ed/2019/the-sad-state-of-happiness-in-the-united-states-and-the-role-of-digital-media/ (accessed on Jan. 20, 2022).

thegoodbook
COMPANY

BIBLICAL | RELEVANT | ACCESSIBLE

At The Good Book Company, we are dedicated to helping Christians and local churches grow. We believe that God's growth process always starts with hearing clearly what he has said to us through his timeless word—the Bible.

Ever since we opened our doors in 1991, we have been striving to produce Bible-based resources that bring glory to God. We have grown to become an international provider of user-friendly resources to the Christian community, with believers of all backgrounds and denominations using our books, Bible studies, devotionals, evangelistic resources, and DVD-based courses.

We want to equip ordinary Christians to live for Christ day by day, and churches to grow in their knowledge of God, their love for one another, and the effectiveness of their outreach.

Call us for a discussion of your needs or visit one of our local websites for more information on the resources and services we provide.

Your friends at The Good Book Company

thegoodbook.com | thegoodbook.co.uk
thegoodbook.com.au | thegoodbook.co.nz
thegoodbook.co.in